HAKE'S
GUIDE TO
COWBOY CHARACTER
COLLECTIBLES

AN ILLUSTRATED PRICE
GUIDE COVERING 50 YEARS OF
MOVIE & TV COWBOY HEROES

TED HAKE

WALLACE-HOMESTEAD BOOK COMPANY
RADNOR, PENNSYLVANIA

NOTICE

Values for items pictured in this book are based on the author's experience as well as actual prices realized for specific items sold through the catalogues of Hake's Americana & Collectibles mail and phone bid auctions. The prices are offered in this book for information purposes only. Many factors, including condition and rarity of the item, geographic location, and the knowledge and opinions of both buyers and sellers influence prices asked and prices paid. As the prices in this book are approximations, neither the author nor the publisher shall be held responsible for any losses that may occur through the use of this book in the purchase or sale of items.

CHARACTER COPYRIGHTS AND TRADEMARKS

For each illustrated item, and in the text of the book, we have acknowledged and identified the copyright holder and/or licensee wherever possible.

Items pictured (top to bottom) in reduced form on the front cover are: Wanted—Dead or Alive "Mare's Laig" Rifle Pistol by Marx, c. 1960, © Four Star-Malcolm, $250; Tom Mix Comics Book 1, © 1940 Ralston-Purina Co., $400; Roy Rogers Forty Niner Pistol and Spurs, c. 1950, © M. A. Henry Limited, $600; The Lone Ranger National Defenders Secret Portfolio, © 1941 General Mills, Inc., $200; Tom Mix Draw and Paint book, © 1935 Whitman Publishing Co., $75; Gene Autry Repeating Cap Pistol by Kenton Hardware, c. 1930s, © Mitchell J. Hamilburg Co., $300; Walt Disney's Official Davy Crockett coonskin hat c. 1955, © Walt Disney Productions, $100; Hopalong Cassidy radio by Arvin Industries, Inc., c. 1950, © Wm. Boyd, $300; Lone Ranger Ring-Toss by Rosebud Art Co., © 1946, The Lone Ranger, Inc., $175; Gene Autry composition figure, c. 1930s, © Gene Autry, $400; Roy Rogers Trick Lasso store display by Knox-Reese Co., 1949, © Roy Rogers, $1200; Bonanza Model Kit by Revell, Inc., © 1966 National Broadcasting Co. Inc., $60; Hopalong Cassidy 25″ tall doll (unmarked) by Ideal Toy Corp., 1949 © Wm. Boyd, $750; Davy Crockett cookie jar by Regal China, 1955, © C. Miller, $400.

Items pictured (left to right) in reduced form on the back cover are: Roy Rogers & Trigger alarm clock by Ingraham Co., 1951, © Roy Rogers, $300; All Star Dairy Products store clock by Advertising Products, Inc., c. 1950, © Wm. Boyd, $1500; Gene Autry Watch by Wilane Watch Co., © 1948 Gene Autry, $400.

We regret any omissions caused by error or the absence of identifying information on any item.

Copyright © 1994 by Ted Hake
All Rights Reserved
Published in Radnor, Pennsylvania 19089, by Wallace-Homestead,
a division of Chilton Book Company

No part of this book may be reproduced, transmitted, or stored
in any form or by any means, electronic, or mechanical,
without prior written permission from the publisher.

Cover and color photography by Mark Jenkins
Cover design by Anthony Jacobson

Manufactured in the United States of America

Library of Congress Cataloging-in-Publication Data
Hake, Theodore L.
   [Guide to cowboy character collectibles]
   Hake's guide to cowboy character collectibles:an illustrated
price guide covering 50 years of movie & TV cowboy heroes / Ted
Hake.
     p.   cm.
   Includes bibliographical references and index.
   ISBN 0-87069-647-5 (pbk.)
   1. Western films—Collectibles. 2. Westerns (Television
programs)—Collectibles. I. Title.
PN1995.9.W4H28   1994
791.45′72—dc20
                       93-41907
                        CIP

1 2 3 4 5 6 7 8 9 0   3 2 1 0 9 8 7 6 5 4

CONTENTS

MOVIE AND TV COWBOY HEROES

APPENDIX

COLOR PAGES

Tom Mix
Gene Autry
The Lone Ranger
Roy Rogers
Hopalong Cassidy
1950s Western Stars
1960s TV Cowboys
Pin-back Buttons & Premiums

ACKNOWLEDGMENTS

I wish to express my gratitude to my staff at Hake's Americana for their assistance: Deak Stagemyer, Joan Carbaugh, Alex Winter and Vonnie Burkins. Special thanks go to Russ King and Jeff Robison for many hours devoted to research, photography and lay-out. My appreciation also to my wife Jonell, my son Ted, and the entire Wallace-Homestead staff for their support and contributions. My friend and cowboy hero collector, Joseph Cywinski, provided valuable assistance in confirming dates and titles.

INTRODUCTION

As late as 1876, the centennial year of the United States, the nation was still geographically two "separate" entities. The eastern half consisted of 31 established states with a significant population. Westward lay a scattered nine states admitted to the Union plus nine "Territories" awaiting significant settlement, let alone population. Estimates are that less than two million people lived throughout the vast western sector. Of this number, estimates are that only some 50,000 (about the current population of Cheyenne, Wyoming) or less were "cowboys" by traditional definition. Further, the true "Old Wild West" era is generally considered to have existed only from the mid-1860s to the mid-1880s. This limited number of cattle hands and their brief 20-year heyday, however, generated a wealth of U.S. western history, lore and the romanticized cowboy hero image in the minds of Easterners.

Cowboy heroes have been a mainstay of several popular entertainment industries, notably latter 19th century pulp magazines through 20th century movies, Big Little Books, radio and subsequent television programming. This reference is not an attempted listing of all cowboy heroes and their memorabilia. Rather, it is an overview of the collectibles produced in consequential amounts for cowboy heroes of mass popularity. These, of course, stem almost entirely from the mass medium periods of movies, radio and TV. In this respect Hake's Guide to Cowboy Character Collectibles is an expansion of our 1976 reference *Six-Gun Heroes* co-authored with Robert D. Cauler, which concentrated basically on movie cowboys and, as applicable, the television years that followed for them.

Television ushered in a host of other western shows throughout the 1950s and early 1960s (see listing at rear of book). These series, whether based on actual cowboy heroes or introducing new fictional ones, created another dimension of cowboy collecting. Today, about 30 years after the peak of TV westerns, the scope and extent of collectibles from that time have become well defined as to identity and quantity vs. scarcity. We hope you enjoy this extensive sampling of cowboy hero collectibles, both as a nostalgia and pricing reference.

USING THIS BOOK

Collectibles related to 64 cowboy heroes are pictured, described and evaluated. A total of over 1,700 collectibles are included. All have been offered in previous Hake's Americana & Collectibles mail and phone bid auctions with the exception of several items currently in inventory for future auctions. The collectibles are selected as a representative sampling for the particular individual, and omission of an item known for that individual does not imply either an abundance or scarcity of that item. Contents are organized as follows:

NAME: Entries are alphabetized according to the individual's first name or first word of the title in the instance of a television series (excluding prefix words ''A'' and ''The'').

DESCRIPTIONS: Quotation marks indicate words or numbers actually appearing on the item (or its packaging) although packaging may not appear in the photo example. A size dimension that involves a fraction is expressed in decimal rather than fraction form, e.g., $10\frac{1}{2}''$ expressed as 10.5''; sizes of larger items may be rounded to the nearest inch. Color or colors of a particular item are indicated only when the color(s) are essential, usually to differentiate from a similar example that may otherwise appear indentical.

ITEM DATES: The actual issue date is used when indicated on the item itself or known from other sources. A ''c.'' for circa (approximate) date is supplied when the item is undated.

PRICES: While all collectibles shown have been offered (excluding a few in current inventory) in Hake's Americana & Collectibles mail and phone bid auction catalogues, the prices indicated are not auction ''prices realized'' for several reasons. Some items in every auction go unsold while some are subject to intense bidding by two or three bidders. The price estimates in this book are based on a combination of factors, including the author's experience, auction prices realized, sales lists and typical prices at collectibles shows. Prices assume the item is in excellent, complete condition without damage or significant wear. If an item is illustrated with a box or other packaging, the price reflects this fact. The same item, even in excellent condition, may have a value of 25 to 50 percent less if the box or packaging is missing.

IMPORTANT: Prices specified are retail prices. Dealers will pay a percentage of these prices based on the quality of the material and their individual business practices.

ABBREVIATIONS:

c. = circa	cello. = celluloid
bw = black and white	br = black and red
bwr = black, white and red	rw = red and white
bwbl = black, white and blue	rwb = red, white and blue

TYPES OF COWBOY HERO COLLECTIBLES

Movie posters, lobby cards, pressbooks and other movie advertising paper items are the earliest collectibles related to specific cowboy heroes. Vending machine photo portrait cards by the Exhibit Supply Co. were also produced for most of the 1920s western movie stars, but the silent movie era produced few other collectibles to document the popularity of the era's cowboy heroes.

Merchandising the cowboy hero began to gain momentum in the early 1930s. Disney's Mickey Mouse showed the way with a licensing program directed by Kay Kamen to put Mickey's image and endorsement on hundreds of products. Although never as successful as Mickey, western movie stars such as Tom Mix, Hoot Gibson, Ken Maynard and Buck Jones began endorsing products such as children's western costumes, riding toys, lariats and air rifles. Their movies were converted to a book format as part of the Whitman Publishing Company series of Big Little Books.

While licensed products expanded during the 1930s, radio shows, usually sponsored by cereal or bread companies, were based on the adventures of Tom Mix, Buck Jones, and The Lone Ranger. These promotions and many that followed resulted in hundreds of premiums such as badges, decoders, rings and club manuals that are still immensely popular with today's collectors.

World War II limited the number of cowboy hero collectibles, but post-war prosperity and the establishment of television set the stage for the cowboy hero world's mightiest merchandiser— William Boyd, a.k.a. Hopalong Cassidy. In 1950, Hoppy appeared on everything from potato chip cans to linoleum floor coverings to children's underwear.

The 1950s offer the widest variety of cowboy hero collectibles. Popularity of the western theme extended across the movies, radio, TV and comic books. From licensed merchandise to premiums, if a youngster could consume, play with, or somehow use a product, most likely something was available with a cowboy hero tie-in.

For collectors, the overwhelming amount of material available forces some specialization. The two most popular approaches are to collect everything associated with a favorite character (or show) or to concentrate on a favorite type of item such as badges, gun sets, or lunch boxes. Whatever the choice, cowboy hero memorabila offers graphically appealing collectibles with enduring popularity.

AVAILABILITY

Cowboy items, particularly those prior to the 1950s, are no longer commonly found at bargain prices on open markets such as antiques shows, co-op shops or flea markets. Exceptions occur, of course, and collectors should not necessarily disregard these sources. Prospective collectors may well find greater satisfaction and expediency through specialized collectible shows, paper memorabilia dealers, or auctions such as ours which offer items selected and obtained on the basis of known desirability to collectors.

Items from the TV era are obviously more recent and can still be found to some extent on the open market, including yard or garage sales, although seldom in complete original state and/or condition.

A number of publications and fan clubs (see appendix) have developed over the past 15 years as collectors with similar interests joined together across the country. Some groups have a very general focus while others are very specific, but all may serve as resources for information and contacts. A good first step is to write (including a self-addressed, stamped envelope) to inquire if a sample of the organization's publication is available. We also welcome inquiries to Hake's Americana & Collectibles, P.O. Box 1444D, York, PA 17405.

CONDITION

Condition cannot be overstressed as a plus factor in collecting, buying, or selling cowboy collectibles, a truism for all mass-produced collectibles. Wear and damage obviously detract from an item's appearance and value. A closely related factor is completeness. All original parts or pieces, in original clean box or packaging, greatly enhances the item's collectible desirability.

Among cowboy collectibles, paper items are most prone to wear. Paper and cardboard items such as movie posters and lobby cards are very likely to have edge and corner wear, including splits and tears. Similar wear often occurs along fold creases if the item is folded, although most larger paper items, principally posters, were folded originally upon publication. Other typical defects of paper items are crude tape repairs, ink markings, pencil erasure marks, loss of surface paper, tack holes, insect damage, brittleness, age browning, and stain from smoke, dust or moisture. Substances other than paper—fabric, metals, leather, celluloid, plaster, rubber, vinyls and plastics—are all subject to their particular types of condition problems due to the aging process and/or heavy use. Truly "mint condition" items among cowboy and other collectibles are rarely found; but collectors should rightfully expect an item to be in reasonably nice condition before considering purchase.

The following terms and definitions are used to describe items in Hake's Americana & Collectibles auctions. These definitions are fairly standard throughout the collectibles hobby, although some dealers, who do not describe each item in detail, have adopted a shorthand system wherein the letter "C" for "Condition" and a number from 1 to 10 is used to designate condition. In this system "C10" equals "mint," "C9" equals "near mint" and so on. The system used at Hake's Americana is:

Mint: Flawless condition. Usually applied to items made of metal or items that are boxed or otherwise packaged. MIB stands for "Mint in box."

Near Mint (NM): Just the slightest detectable wear but appearance is still like new.

Excellent (Exc.): Only the slightest detectable wear, if any at all. Usually applied to buttons, paper and other non-metallic items. Also used for metallic items that just miss the near mint or mint level.

Very Fine (VF): Bright clean condition. An item that has seen little use and was well cared for with only very minor wear or aging.

Fine: An item in nice condition with some general wear but no serious defects.

Very Good (VG): Shows use but no serious defect and still nice for display. Metal items may have detail or paint wear. Paper items may have some small tears or creases.

Good: May have some obvious overall wear and/or some specific defect but still with some collectible value.

Fair: Obvious damage to some extent.

Poor: Extensive damage or wear.

At Hake's we grade our items conservatively; less than 1% of the 20,000 items we sell annually are returned due to an error in describing the item's condition. However, in the collectibles business much wishful thinking occurs regarding condition, particularly by less experienced dealers and among the general public attempting to sell items found around the house. When purchasing items through the mail, it is best to have a clear understanding with the seller that the item can be returned for a refund if the item has more wear or damage than the seller specified.

PRICES

Cowboy hero collectibles have been featured in Hake's auctions since our first catalogue in 1967. Today, the collector's response to prices of items in that era is, "I'll take a dozen." Values have increased dramatically since the days when we were establishing the groundwork for America's popular culture collectibles business.

Unchanged is the dictum that prices are established by supply and demand. These two paramount criteria are influenced by:

1. CONDITION—wear and damage quickly reduce an item's potential value. Few examples of items meant to be used, usually by children, survive in truly "mint" condition. Demand for and scarcity of "mint" items results in a high premium price for items in flawless condition. The collector who can emotionally accept an item in less than "mint" condition has a powerful bargaining chip and can often acquire items that are visually perfect for a fraction of the cost required for a "mint" example.

2. COMPLETENESS—missing parts or pages, instruction sheets and original packaging all result in price reductions. Original boxes are particularly valued and can often double the value compared to an unboxed example of the same item.

3. DESIGN FEATURES—aesthetics influence value. Items made of quality materials, designed with appealing graphics or some unique feature, will result in higher demand and command a higher value.

4. CROSSOVER INTEREST—many items appeal to several distinct collector groups. Both a radio collector and a Hopalong Cassidy collector would desire the Hoppy radio resulting in higher dealer prices or hotly contested auction bidding.

5. RARITY—with nearly 30 years in the collectibles business, we have a good knowledge of what is rare and we have shared this perspective with our bidders and readers through auctions and price guides. However, we have seen time after time that rarity must be combined with demand to produce any significant increase in an item's value.

6. DISTRIBUTION—cowboy hero items can be found throughout the country. Prices tend to be a bit higher on the east and west coasts where there are larger concentrations of people looking for similar items.

7. EMOTIONS—there are no exact prices for cowboy hero collectibles. Personal opinions about rarity, desirability and condition, on the part of both the seller and buyer, determine the prices asked and prices paid. To make informed purchases, the collector should study price guides, review auction results, attend shows, join clubs, subscribe to useful publications, and communicate with fellow collectors.

REPRODUCTIONS

As collectibles become valuable, each hobby is plagued by unethical people who produce undated reproductions and fantasy (recently created) items. The field of cowboy collectibles has a small number of these spurious items, but the collector can acquaint himself with these rather easily.

Some movie posters and lobby cards have been reproduced, but with a little study these are generally recognizable because the color inks and paper stocks do not exactly match the originals. Other movie posters and lobby cards, although legitimate, were reissued at a later date for the re-release of an earlier film. These reissues often, but not always, have an ''R'' designation next to a date along the bottom margin.

Inexperienced collectors can best assure themselves of original items by buying from reputable dealers who do not sell any type of fraudulent collectibles and who unconditionally guarantee their items as authentic.

Here is a list of some frequently encountered cowboy hero reproduction (R) and fantasy (F) collectibles:

Tom Mix

(F) Brass Star Badge. 6 points showing crossed pistols and inscribed ''TOM MIX & TONY.''

(R) Club Manual. For Ralston Straight Shooters, 1945, showing covered wagon on cover with ''TM'' brand in red. Original has blank inside covers, reproduction inside covers picture ''TOM MIX AND TONY'' (front) and Curley Bradley with guitar (back).

The Lone Ranger

(R) Button. 1″ inscribed ''SUNDAY HERALD AND EXAMINER.'' The original is lithographed tin, the reproduction is celluloid covered.

(R) Metal Badge. 1″ silvered metal with blue background paint showing The Lone Ranger riding Silver. Issued for members of club sponsored by ''SILVERCUP'' bread. The original has pin soldered directly to reverse, the reproduction has pin running through a slotted oval metal plate.

Gene Autry

(R) Button. 1¼″ with black-and-white photo on blue background. Text reads ''GENE AUTRY'S BRAND/Sunbeam Bread.'' Original has ''GENE AUTRY'' name and copyright symbol on curl. Metal back has embossed ''UNION LABEL/Local 115/SHOP NO. 2.'' Reproduction has neither of the preceding markings.

(R) Button. 1¼″ with photo and text in black and white and rim in orange and white. Text reads ''Gene Autry/OFFICIAL GENE AUTRY CLUB BADGE.'' Curl text reads ''ECONOMY NOVELTY & PRINTING CO., N.Y.C.'' Reproduction has no text on the curl.

Hopalong Cassidy

(F) Bandanna. Yellow fabric with heavy black ink image of Hoppy riding Topper printed on one corner.

(F) Brass Star Badge. 6 points with words ''HOPALONG CASSIDY'' on two curved lines above and below the word ''SHERIFF.''

(F) Pencil Sharpener. Yellow plastic 1″ round by ½″ thick with black image of Hoppy and ''HOPALONG CASSIDY'S SAVING RODEO/TENDERFOOT.''

(F) Button. 1½″ lithographed tin with black-and-white illustration of Hoppy on bright yellow background. Text reads "QUALITY DAIRY/My Favorite/ICE CREAM/Hopalong Cassidy/ QUALITY DAIRY CO., ST. LOUIS, MISSOURI."

(R) Hopalong Cassidy Savings Club. Original buttons in this series are lithographed tin, reproductions are celluloid covered. The reproduction 3″ size button is often sold in a glassine bag.

(R) Silvered Metal Star Badge. 6 points inscribed "HOPALONG CASSIDY" with embossed portrait at center. Original has pin attached to folded over narrow metal strip, reproduction has pin mounted on 3/16″ wide metal bar soldered horizontally across the reverse.

Roy Rogers/Dale Evans
(F) Pencil Sharpener. Blue and white plastic 1″ round by ½″ thick with portrait of "ROY ROGERS" surrounded by a horseshoe.

(F) Buttons. 1 3/4″ full color portrait of "ROY ROGERS" on gray background. There is a matching "DALE EVANS." Seen without back paper but also with glued-in copy of a back paper with the "BASTIAN BROS." name as manufacturer plus a jobber's name and address of "HARGREAVES PRINTING CO. 245 MAIN ST., DALLAS, TEXAS, AGENTS."

(R) Pocketwatch. Similar to original but dial is a color photocopy.

(R) Brass Star Badge. 6 points with "ROY ROGERS DEPUTY SHERIFF" surrounding portraits of Roy and Trigger. Original has red plastic whistle and signaling device on reverse, reproduction reverse only has brass pin running through slotted oval metal plate.

COLLECTING TIPS

SOURCES—in a local area, cowboy collectibles may be found at garage sales, estate auctions, local shops, flea markets or antiques shows. Friends and relatives may help in the quest and some collectors try advertising in local newspapers. If you can travel, there are probably more specialized shows within reach. Most cowboy collectibles will turn up at toy shows, but don't overlook shows and collector conventions devoted to dolls, tin containers, advertising, paper collectibles and other specialties because cowboy collectibles cover such a wide variety of items. You can cover the entire country by mail and telephone. Clubs and publications (see appendix) will put you in touch with shows, dealer sales lists and telephone bid auctions.

SPECIALIZE—think about your collecting goal before engaging in an unfocused buying spree. Eventually, money or space limitations force some degree of specialization on nearly every collector. A collection built around a well-defined theme containing items in very fine or better condition will yield a financial advantage when the time comes to sell.

PRESERVATION—includes the important considerations of care, storage and security. Cowboy collectibles are tangible artifacts of our cultural heritage. Hopefully, the collector will preserve the items and protect them from damage while serving as caretaker. Writing on items with pencil or pen, applying adhesive stickers, and covering tears with tape are not proper conservation methods. Prices or notes can be made on separate papers, stickers can go on protective coverings, rather than the item, and nonstaining archival paper tape can be used on damaged paper. Linen mounting is recommended for large paper items such as posters. Sometimes restoration or repair is necessary to make an item attractive or workable, but the collector should invest time in learning the proper procedures or else turn the job over to a professional.

Other perils to collections include dust, smoke, moisture and sunlight. Glass cases for three-dimensional items can overcome the dangers of soiling and yellowing from dust and smoke. The same is true for glass framing of paper items. Drapes can block bright sunlight to eliminate fading. In most environments, housing a collection in the living area will be enough to avoid the dangers of excessive heat, cold, moisture and silverfish found in attics and basements.

Glass frames, known as Riker mounts, work well for the flat storage of celluloid button collections; however, if the lining in the bottom tray is cotton, in high humidity areas the cotton will attract moisture that will extensively damage the backs of buttons before any signs of damage appear on the front. Litho buttons may adhere to the glass and lose paint when removed. Many button collectors also use plastic sheets with pockets designed to hold coins. This works provided litho buttons are not placed in the sheets. Some sheets contain chemicals that react with the inks on the buttons to virtually melt the ink after a period of time. If these sheets are used at all, they should be stored vertically rather than flat to keep the accumulated weight off the bottom sheets.

The best place for storing both celluloid and litho buttons and other small items is in a cabinet with stacks of shallow drawers. Such cabinets are available (they are also favored by coin collectors). The cabinet provides darkness and protection from dust and smoke, there is no pressure on the objects, and the doors can be locked for security.

Proper security is always a matter of personal judgment. To some, the prevailing security of the dwelling itself is adequate. Others may opt for the security of safety deposit boxes offered by banks, although this obviously hinders casual enjoyment. Some insurance companies offer specialized policies against theft or other loss, although most will require a detailed inventory listing and/or a professional appraisal of monetary value before underwriting a collectibles policy.

THE FUTURE

Cowboy hero collectibles have long been a firmly established segment of the overall collectibles marketplace. In fact, over the past two years interest has never been stronger in movie and TV cowboy collectibles of the 1960s and earlier. The number of bidders on cowboy collectibles in our auctions has reached record numbers. Even television, which largely ignored western/cowboy themes for much of the 1970s and 1980s, has rediscovered the public's enduring fondness of the genre and produced several series and TV movies for the 1993-94 seasons. While these newest media offerings have not produced any collectibles we are aware of, that could change quickly. Even if that does not happen, ever expanding cable TV channels and video tape offerings expose young, new audiences to the popular cowboy heroes of the past. As America heads into the 21st century, it seems certain cowboy hero collectibles will continue to be treasured as artifacts of our national fascination with the West.

The Adventures Of Rin-Tin-Tin

Rin-Tin-Tin, also known by shorter Rinty and Rinny, was among the first and certainly the most durable of wonder dog heroes, dating from 1920s Warner Bros. silent films through a very popular 1950s TV series. Ever the epitome of a quick-thinking German Shepard, Rinty was the ward in the television version of the 101st Cavalry, known as The Fighting Blue Devils, based at Fort Apache, Arizona Territory. The original series consisted of 164 episodes on ABC-TV beginning October 15, 1954 through August 28, 1959.

1

2

3

4

5

6

7

8

1
"KEN-L-RATION" 5x7" bw dog food premium photo w/facsimile signature including name of trainer Lee Duncan and 1931 date. $20

2
"KEN-L-BISKIT" 3.75x3.75x.75" dog food sample box w/1932 issue date. $30

3
"RIN-TIN-TIN" 4x8x11" tall painted plaster figure with rhinestone eyes c. 1930s. $75

4
"THE LONE DEFENDER" 3x7" bw cardboard ink blotter for un-dated but 1930 serial movie. $25

5
"THE FAMOUS FILM DOG" 3.5x5.5" bw card #259 from English "Picturegoer" series c. 1930s. $15

6
"MONTE BLUE & RIN TIN TIN" 3.5x5.5" monochrome card c. 1930s. $15

7
RIN-TIN-TIN .75x1.5x2.5" tall color matchbox with Spanish inscription for cigar c. 1930s. $35

8
"CHILDREN'S PLAYMATE" 6x9" monthly magazine for January 1958. $15

9
"ADVENTURES OF RIN-TIN-TIN" 9x17.5x1.5" boxed Transogram board game copyright 1955. $75

9

10
"TV GUIDE" 5x7.5" weekly issue for July 2, 1955 with cover article also related to Lassie. $25

11
RODEO 8x11" program from Boston Garden 1956. $30

12
"DOG CARE" 7x10" book by Rinty's trainer Lee Duncan © 1958. $20

13
RIN TIN TIN 8.5x10.5" Whitman coloring book © 1955. $20

14
RIN TIN TIN 8.5x10.5" Whitman coloring book © 1957. $20

15
RINTY AND RUSTY 5.5x6.5" Whitman book © 1957. $15

16
RIN TIN TIN 8.5x11" Golden Press book © 1958. $20

17
RIN-TIN-TIN 6.5 × 8" Little Golden Book © 1957. $15

18
RIN TIN TIN 6x8" Whitman book © 1958. $15

19
"MARCH OF COMICS" 5x7.25" retail store premium booklet © 1957. $20

20
RIN-TIN-TIN 12x12.25" cardboard album holding 33 1/3 rpm Columbia Record mid-1950s. $15

21
"RINTY BREAKS THROUGH" 10x10" cardboard album holding 78 rpm Columbia record © 1955. $25

22
RIN TIN TIN 12.25x12.25" cardboard album holding 33 1/3 rpm Columbia record © 1955. $30

23
"LT. RIP MASTERS" 7x7" paper album holding 45 rpm MGM record by James Brown mid-1950s. $30

10

11

12

13

14

15

16

17

18

19

20

21

22

23

24

25

26

27

28

29

30

31

32

33

24
''RIN TIN TIN'' 9.5x14″ cardboard centered by magic slate film drawing board c. mid-1950s. $30

25
''YO HO RINTY'' 10.5x11″ vinyl over cardboard notebook cover © 1957. $35

26
''RUSTY—RIN-TIN-TIN'' 3.5″ steel pocketknife with blw plastic side panels including Morse Code on reverse panel c. mid-1950s. $50

27
RUSTY/RINTY 7x9x2″ deep boxed Whitman jigsaw puzzle c. mid-1950s. $20

28
RINTY/RUSTY 11.5x14.5″ Whitman frame tray inlay jigsaw puzzle c. 1955. $20

29
''RIN TIN TIN RING'' 6x7.25″ color back panel from Nabisco Rice Honeys cereal box that held one of the 12 pictured rings c. 1954-1956. $60

30
''RIN TIN TIN TOTEM POLE'' set of eight 2x5.5″ embossed color punch-out cards issued as Nabisco box inserts c. 1954-1956. EACH $8

31
RIN TIN TIN 2.5x2.5″ paper pull-off color sticker patches issued as set of seven Nabisco cereal box inserts © 1958. EACH $8

32
''RUSTY'' 8.5x11x3.5″ deep boxed fabric masquerade costume and vinyl mask by Ben Cooper, Inc. c. mid-1950s. $65

33
''WONDA-SCOPE'' 1.75″ dia. plastic case magnetic compass that also has signal mirror and binocular lenses, Nabisco premium c. 1954-1956. $30

34
"RIN TIN TIN" 3x4.5" mailing envelope and 1 3/8" color lithographed tin button for entrant in Nabisco "Name The Puppy" contest c. 1956. PACKAGED $40, BUTTON ONLY $15

34

35
"RIN TIN TIN" 5x5" long plastic retractable "Rifle Pen" in 3x6x.5" Nabisco mailing box c. 1954-1956. BOXED $40, PEN ONLY $20

36
"RIN-TIN-TIN AND RUSTY" 8" long metal and plastic revolver in black leather holster. Belt is matching leather with embossed portrait metal buckle. Nabisco premium c. 1954-1956. GUN, $75, HOLSTER $50

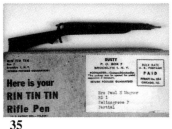

35   **36**

37
"RUSTY 101 CAVALRY" 9x9" thin plastic Nabisco premium mask c. 1954-1956. $25

38
"FIGHTING BLUE DEVILS 101st CAVALRY" 13x5" tall blue felt premium hat by Nabisco c. 1954-1956. $50

37   **38**

39
"101st CAVALRY" 7" tall brown hard vinyl canteen with threaded cap plus vinyl carrying strap, Nabisco premium © 1957. $20

40
"101st CAVALRY" 6.25x8.5" blue felt banner inked in yellow, Nabisco premium c. 1954-1956. $25

41
RIN TIN TIN 8x10" glossy bw TV cast member photo with facsimile signatures, Nabisco premium c. 1955. $30

39   **40**   **41**

42
RIN TIN TIN 4" wide plastic viewer with set of 24 stereo image picture cards, each 2x4". Nabisco premium c. 1954-1956. VIEWER $30, EACH CARD $3

43
RIN TIN TIN 4x4.5" View-Master reel set © 1955. $25

42   **43**

Allan (Rocky) Lane (1904–1973)

Lane (real name Harry Albershart) began his film career in the 1930s but was not well known for cowboy roles until succeeding Bill Elliott in the Red Ryder series circa 1944. He emerged from the series about four years later with the studio-added "Rocky" nickname plus horse Black Jack to become a star in his own right, about 50 films in all. He was one of Republic's last big western stars until the demise of that studio's major cowboy films in 1953. His 1938–1961 acting career consisted of 59 western film credits. Lane also provided the voice of the talking horse for TV's *Mister Ed* series.

1

2

3

4

5

6

7

8   **9**

1
"ROCKY LANE" 7.25x9.75" English "Western Comic Annual No. 3" of bw comic strips, undated early 1950s. $20

2
"ROCKY LANE WESTERN" 7x10.25" Fawcett Vol. 4 #20 comic book for December 1950. $40

3
BOWMAN GUM "PRE-VUE" 2.25x2.5" bw flip booklet #8 from Series 1 of 24 booklets, each designed with pages to be flipped to view sequence scene from Rocky Lane movie "Renegades Of Sonora" of 1948. EACH $12

4
"ALLAN 'ROCKY' LANE" 8x10" Dixie ice cream premium color picture c. early 1950s. $20

5
"ALLAN 'ROCKY' LANE" 8x10" Dixie ice cream premium color picture c. early 1950s. $20

6
"BANDITS OF THE WEST" 27x41" paper poster for 1953 Republic Picture. $40

7
"SUNDOWN IN SANTA FE" 27x41" paper poster for 1948 Republic Picture. $35

8
"CAPTIVE OF BILLY THE KID" 11x14" color lobby card for 1951 Republic Picture. $12

9
"GUNMEN OF ABILENE" 11x14" color lobby card for 1950 Republic Picture. $12

Annie Oakley

An actual female sharpshooter (real name Mrs. Phoebe Ann Butler) of the late 19th century whose feats included "Little Sure Shot" performances in Buffalo Bill Cody's touring Wild West Show beginning in 1885. A 1935 RKO movie, *Annie Oakley*, starred Barbara Stanwyck and a 1950 *Annie Get Your Gun* film version of the Broadway musical starred Betty Hutton. The TV adventure series starred Gail Davis, a frequent Western film starlet of the late 1940s and early 1950s. The series, the first TV western to star a woman, was produced by Gene Autry Flying A Productions and consisted of 81 episodes from 1953 through 1956.

1
"TV GUIDE" 5x7.5" issue for week of July 28, 1956. $20

2
"ANNIE OAKLEY/GAIL DAVIS" autographed 8x10" glossy bw photo c. mid-1950s. $50

3
ANNIE OAKLEY 4x5" bw cast member photo with facsimile signatures c. mid-1950s. $15

4
ANNIE OAKLEY/GAIL DAVIS 8x10" bw glossy photo with facsimile signature c. mid-1950s. $10

5
"DANGER AT DIABLO" 6x8" Whitman book © 1955. $15

6
"ANNIE OAKLEY IN DOUBLE TROUBLE" 6x8" Whitman book © 1958. $15

7
"ANNIE OAKLEY AND TAGG" 7x10.25" first issue Gold Key #1 comic book from 1958. $15

8
"ANNIE OAKLEY CUT-OUT DOLLS" 10.5x13" Whitman book © 1958, example shows both covers. $50

9
"ANNIE OAKLEY WITH TAGG AND LOFTY" 10.5x12.5" Whitman cut-out doll book © 1955, example shows both covers. $50

10
"ANNIE OAKLEY CUT-OUT DOLLS" 10.5x12" Watkins-Strathmore book © 1956. $50

1

2

3

4

5

6

7

8

9

10

11   **12**   **13**

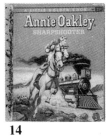

14   **16**

15

17   **18**

19

20

11
"ANNIE OAKLEY" 11x13"
Whitman coloring book © 1957.
$25

12
"ANNIE OAKLEY" 11x13"
Whitman "Roundup Coloring
Book With Lofty And Tagg"
© 1955. $25

13
"ANNIE OAKLEY IN THE
GHOST TOWN SECRET" 6x8"
Whitman book © 1957. $15

14
"ANNIE OAKLEY SHARP-
SHOOTER" 6.75x8" Little
Golden Book © 1956. $10

15
"ANNIE OAKLEY" 5" tall fabric
patch for girl's outfit c. 1955. $15

16
"ANNIE OAKLEY" 4x4" packet
set of three View-Master reels c.
mid-1950s. $15

17
"COWBOYS" 4x5.75" packet set
of three Tru-Vue film cards for
Annie Oakley, Rex Allen, Kit
Carson © 1954 and 1955. $35

18
"FLAMING GUNS" 4x5.5" Tru-
Vue film card © 1955. $12

19
"SPARKLE PICTURE CRAFT"
12x17x1.5" Gabriel boxed kit
© 1955. $40

20
"SEWING SET" 10.5x14x2"
boxed Pressman Toy kit c. 1955-
1956. $50

21
"ANNIE OAKLEY SAYS" 2.5"
color cardboard string tag pin with
front phrase completed on back
"Eat Wonder Bread" c. 1955. $25

22
"ANNIE OAKLEY AND
TAGG" 10x12x3" boxed set of
leather holsters holding cap pistols
by Daisy Mfg. Co. c. 1955. $200

23
ANNIE OAKLEY 9" tall Hartland
Plastics Co. figure with all acces-
sories c. mid-1950s. $100

24
"ANNIE OAKLEY" fabric and
fringe cowgirl skirt with 24" bottom width c. 1955. $25

25
"ANNIE OAKLEY AND
TAGG" 4.5x12" color card holding elastic fabric suspenders c.
1953-1956. $25

26
"ANNIE OAKLEY AND
TAGG" 7x8x3.75" deep steel
lunch box with 6.5" tall bottle by
Aladdin Industries © 1955. BOX
$200, BOTTLE $75

27
"MAGIC ERASABLE PIC-
TURES" 9x10" card with spiral
bound stiff cardboard erasable coloring pages by Transogram
© 1959. $25

28
"ANNIE OAKLEY" 9.5x18.5x2"
boxed board game by Game Gems
© 1965 but based on mid-1950s
TV series. $50

29
"ANNIE OAKLEY" 7x11x2"
boxed Milton Bradley jigsaw puzzle c. 1955. $25

30
"ANNIE OAKLEY SINGS"
6.5x7.5" envelope holding 78 rpm
Little Golden Record c. mid-
1950s. $15

31
"ANNIE OAKLEY SINGS"
6.5x7.5" envelope holding 78 rpm
Little Golden Record c. mid-
1950s. $15

21 **22**

23 **24** **25**

26 **27**

28 **29**

30 **31**

Bat Masterson

A television series based on actual 19th century lawman whose credentials may have been limited to card sharping and friendship with Marshal Wyatt Earp who deputized him for law enforcement in Dodge City. The TV version starred Gene Barry as not only a professional gambler but also as a dapper, urbane, suave attorney whose principal weapon was a gold-tipped cane that disguised a sword. The original series ran on NBC-TV from October 8, 1959 through September 21, 1961. A 1959 United Artists film *The Gunfight At Dodge City* starred Joel McCrea as Masterson.

1

2

3

4

5

6

7

WESTERN 7   Adela Mara and Gene Barry   Printed in U.S.A.

8

9

1
"TV GUIDE" 5x7.5" issue for May 21, 1960. $15

2
"BAT MASTERSON" 2x3.25x9.25" tall boxed 7.5" tall Hartland Plastics Co. figure with accessories c. 1960. BOXED $300, LOOSE $200

3
"BAT MASTERSON" 8.5x11" Saalfield Co. coloring book © 1959. $25

4
"BAT MASTERSON" 6x8" Whitman book © 1960. $15

5
"GENE BARRY" 8x10" auto-graphed glossy color photo c. 1960. $30

6
"BAT MASTERSON" 3.5x4.5" embossed color vinyl wallet c. 1960. $25

7
"BAT MASTERSON" 10x20x2.5" boxed Lowell Toy Corp. game © 1958. $50

8
CARD #7 bw 3.25x5.5" from set of 64 titled "TV Western Stars" by Nu Trading Cards 1960s. $3

9
"BAT MASTERSON" 12x13x4" tall black felt hat with fabric pic-ture label by Arlington Hats c. 1960. $30

Bill Elliott (1903–1965)

A tall, lean and lanky cowboy star (real name Gordon Elliott) whose horse riding talents came naturally from youthful training by his rancher father as well as stockyard cowhands and rodeo performances. His film career began with Warner Bros. in the late 1920s albeit often as a non-Western villain. His 1939 movie, *Taming of the West,* starred him as "Wild Bill Saunders" and the "Wild" nickname stayed with him throughout the rest of his acting career. He is well remembered for his Red Ryder roles and as a very convincing fistfighter. After the disappearance of western movies in the mid-1950s, he starred in several detective-oriented movies. A total of 81 western film credits were amassed between 1928 and 1954.

1
"WILLIAM (BILL) ELLIOTT"
8x10″ color photo 1940s. $20

2
ESKEW'S RODEO 8.5x11″ program featuring acts by Elliott on horse "Stormy" c. 1948. $30

3
"WILD BILL ELLIOTT"
3.5x5.5″ monochrome exhibit card c. 1940s. $8

4
BILL ELLIOTT 2.75″ dia. Dixie ice cream monochrome waxed cardboard cup lid 1940. $12

5
"CALLING WILD BILL ELLIOTT" 2.25″ Dixie ice cream monochrome waxed cardboard cup lid 1943. $15

6
"BILL ELLIOTT" 8x10″ Dixie ice cream color photo 1940. $20

7
"BILL ELLIOTT" 8x10″ Dixie ice cream color picture 1941. $20

8
"BILL ELLIOTT-TEX RITTER"
8x10″ Dixie ice cream color picture 1942. $20

9
"PRAIRIE SCHOONERS"
27x41″ one-sheet color poster for Astor Pictures 1940 film. $60

10
"VENGEANCE OF THE WEST"
27x41″ one-sheet color poster for Columbia Pictures 1942 film. $60

11
"THE SAVAGE HORDE" 27x41″ one-sheet color poster for Republic Pictures 1949 film. $40

1

2

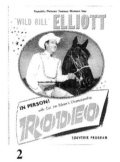
3

4

5

6

7

8

9

10

11

Bobby Benson

The title star of *Bobby Benson's Adventures,* a radio western adventure series begun on CBS in 1932. Bobby was the youthful owner of a south Texas ranch named the H-Bar-O, a not-so-coincidental title in view of program sponsor H-O (Hecker's Oats) Cereal. Bobby and his cowgirl sidekick Polly Armstead were aided by other ranch regulars in encountering and solving local mysteries. When Hecker canceled sponsorship in 1936, the series continued briefly under a new title *Songs of the B-Bar-B* under different cereal sponsorship. The show was revived on Mutual Network in 1949 under yet another title *Bobby Benson and the B-Bar-B Riders.*

Bobby was played in the original years by several individuals. Among the other 1930s cast members were Tex Ritter, comedian Don Knotts as Windy Wales (Teller of Wild Tales), and Al Hodge (later to become Captain Video on TV).

1
BOBBY BENSON 3.5x4.5″ Whitman Big Little Book #1108 © 1934. $35

2
BOBBY BENSON 5.5x8.5″ tinted bw premium photo with facsimile signature c. 1932-1935. $45

3
BOBBY BENSON 7.5x9.25″ bw photo from premium set of nine c. 1932-1935. EACH $10

4
"AFRICA" 18.5x24″ color paper premium map keyed to radio adventures c. 1932-1935. $150

5
"H-O" 22x23x36″ triangular yellow/blue fabric neckerchief c. 1932-1935. $50

6
"RANGER" 1x1.5″ metal badge overlaid by silver/red/black embossed foil art c. 1932-1935. $50

7
"CODE RULE" 2x5″ bw paper slide rule © 1935 by H-O. $50

8
"CODE BOOK" 3x4.5″ companion manual to #7. $40

9
"THE LOST HERD" 5x7″ H-O story booklet © 1936. $15

10
"TUNNEL OF GOLD" 5x7″ H-O story booklet © 1936. $15

11
"B-BAR-B RIDERS" 11x15″ Whitman coloring book based on radio revival show © 1950. $20

Bonanza

One of the new TV shows for the 1959–1960 season, introduced Saturday evening, September 12, *Bonanza* would become the second longest-running western among the dozens of new offerings to follow in the next decade. The show was the engrossing weekly tale of the Cartwrights on the immense Ponderosa Ranch near Virginia City, Nevada.

Lorne Greene starred as the patriarchal three-time widowed father. His sons were half-brothers Adam (Pernell Roberts), Hoss (Dan Blocker), Little Joe (Michael Landon). Although Roberts left the series in 1965, *Bonanza* continued its uninterrupted course totaling over 13 years, second only to *Gunsmoke* in longevity.

1
"TV GUIDE" weekly issue for June 25, 1960. $35

2
"TV MAGAZINE" 5.25x7.25" supplement schedule guide to local newspapers for week of June 11, 1961. $25

3
"NBC-TV" 21x24" stiff paper publicity poster by National Broadcasting Corp. c. 1965. $60

4
"BEN" 2x4x11" boxed 8" tall action figure with accessories from "American Character" series © 1966. $150

5
"LITTLE JOE" from same series as #4. $150

6
"HOSS" from same series as #4. $150

7
"OUTLAW" from same series as #4. $150

8
"BEN AND HIS HORSE" 10x18x3" boxed 8" tall action figure with accessories from "American Character" series © 1966. $250

9
"HOSS AND HIS HORSE" from same series as #8. $250

10
"BONANZA 4 IN 1 WAGON"-boxed accessory set form same series as #8. BOXED WITH ALL ACCESSORIES $250

1

2

3

4

5

6

7

8   9

10

11

12

13

14

15

16

17

11
"BONANZA" 10x10x3" boxed plastic model assembly kit for three characters by Revell Inc. © 1966. BOXED $125, BUILT $60

12
"BONANZA" 7x8x4" deep steel lunch box and 7" steel thermos set by Aladdin Industries c. 1965. BOX $100, BOTTLE $50

13
"BONANZA" 14x14.5x1.25" boxed Parker Brothers "Michigan Rummy" game c. mid-1960s. $30

14
"BONANZA" 7x8x4" deep embossed steel lunch box and 6.5" steel thermos set by Aladdin Industries c. 1968. BOX $125, BOTTLE $50

15
"THE HOSS" 9x13" card holding plastic "Range Pistol" by Marx Toys © 1966. CARDED $125, LOOSE $60

16
"BONANZA" leather double holster set with 9.5" long cap guns by Halpern Co. c. 1965. $175

17
"BONANZA" 10.25x4x1.5" boxed 9.5" metal cap gun Spanish-made by Pilen c. 1960s. BOXED $100, LOOSE $60

18
"BONANZA" 26x5x3.5" boxed 24" cap rifle and 9" cap pistol plus holster and cartridge belt by Marx Toys © 1966. BOXED (NOT SHOWN) $200, LOOSE $100

19
"STARDUST" 12x15x1" boxed "Velvet Art" Craft kit with two pictures © 1965. $50

20
"FOTO FANTASTIKS" 9.5x16.5x1" boxed set of six actual photos featuring Little Joe and materials for coloring them by Eberhard Faber Co. c. 1966. $135

21
"FOTO FANTASTIKS" kit from same series as #20 featuring Ben Cartwright photos. $135

22
"BONANZA" 12x25x2" boxed woodburning kit including eight wood plaques © 1965. $250

23
"BONANZA" 12.5x12.5" cardboard album holding 33 1/3 rpm "Ponderosa Party Time" record on RCA Victor label © 1962. $60

24
"LORNE GREENE" 8x10" school tablet with color cover c. late 1960s. $35

25
LITTLE JOE/MICHAEL LANDON 8x10" color photo c. early 1960s. $25

26
"BONANZA" 10.5x14" Saalfield Co. frame tray inlay jigsaw puzzle © 1963. $40

27
"BONANZA" 5.5x7.5" color card holding plastic viewer and two boxed films © 1961. $50

28
"BONANZA" 4.5x4.5" View-Master pack © 1964. $40

29
"BONANZA" 4.5x4.5" View-Master pack © 1971. $35

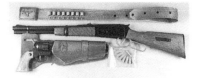

18

19

20

21

22

23

24

25

26

27

28

29

30

31

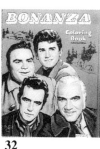

32

33

34

35

36

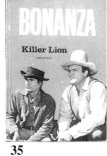

37

38

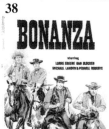

39

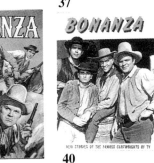

40

41

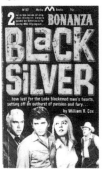

42

43

30
"BONANZA" 10.5x13.5" issue of Saturday Evening Post for December 4, 1965. $15

31
"BONANZA" 8.5x11" first issue picture and song folio by Twin Hits Inc. © 1965. $50

32
"BONANZA" 8.5x11" Saalfield Co. coloring book © 1960. $25

33
"BONANZA" 8.25x11" Saalfield Co. coloring book © 1965. $20

34
"BONANZA" 8.5x11" Saalfield coloring book © 1967. $50

35
"KILLER LION" 5.5x7.75" Whitman book © 1966. $15

36
"TREACHERY TRAIL" 6x8" Whitman book © 1968. $15

37
"BONANZA" 7.25x10" English comic strip book © 1962. $70

38
"BONANZA" 8.25x11" English comic strip book © 1962. $60

39
"BONANZA" 7.5x10.5" English comic strip book © 1963. $50

40
"BONANZA" 8x11" English storybook © 1964. $50

41
"BONANZA" 7.5x10.5" English comic strip book © 1965. $50

42
"BLACK SILVER" 4.25x7" Media Books paperback © 1967. $15

43
"PONDEROSA RANCH" 1x4x5" boxed double set of playing cards c. 1965-1966. $50

44
''BONANZA'' 5x7" photo card
early 1960s. $35

45
BONANZA 5x7" photo card of
three cast members c. 1966. $20

46
''PONDEROSA RANCH'' 4" dia.
metal ashtray late 1960s. $50

47
BEN CARTWRIGHT 8x11" pine
wood plaque c. 1960s. $50

48
HOSS CARTWRIGHT 8x11" pine
wood plaque c. 1960s. $50

49
''THE PONDEROSA RANCH
STORY'' 6x9" color booklet c.
1966. $40

50
''PONDEROSA RANCH'' 2.75"
tall tin cup picturing four cast
members with reverse image of
ranch house plus stagecoach in
foreground c. 1964. $40

51
''PONDEROSA RANCH'' 2.75"
tall tin cup picturing ranch house
with reverse image same as #50,
probably second version c. 1964.
$30

52
''PONDEROSA RANCH'' 2.75"
tall tin cup picturing three figures
with reverse image of ranch house
and flatbed trailer carrying tourists
in foreground c. 1966. $20

53
''BEN CARTWRIGHT'S PON-
DEROSA RANCH'' 2.75" tall tin
cup with reverse image same as
#52 except most of trailer image
is deleted. c. 1966. $30

54
''BONANZA DAYS'' 3" rwb button c. 1964. $75

55
''I LIKE ADAM'' 2.5" tin stickpin early 1960s. $50

56
''I LIKE JOE'' 2.5" tin stickpin
early 1960s. $75

44

45

46

47   **48**

49

50

51   **52**

53   **54**

55   **56**

Brave Eagle

A short-lived but unusual TV series of western adventure from the American Indian viewpoint of Brave Eagle (Keith Larsen), young chief of the Cheyennes, confronted by white man's encroachments of land. Other major cast members were Morning Star (Kim Winona), Keena (Keena Nomkeena), both of actual Indian heritage. The show began on CBS-TV September 28, 1955 and concluded June 6, 1956.

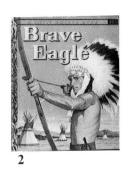

1

3

4

5

1
"BRAVE EAGLE" 8.5x11" Whitman coloring book authorized by Roy Rogers Enterprises © 1955. $25

2
"BRAVE EAGLE" 6.5x8" Simon & Schuster Little Golden Book © 1957. $15

3
"BRAVE EAGLE" 6.25x8.5x3.75" deep steel lunch box by American Thermos c. 1957. BOX $200, BOTTLE (NOT SHOWN) $100

4
"BRAVE EAGLE" 8x10x4" boxed 12-piece set featuring painted plastic figure under Roy Rogers-Frontiers Inc. © 1956. BOXED $200, LOOSE $100

5
"BRAVE EAGLE AND WHITE CLOUD" 8.5x9.25x3" deep boxed set with accessories by Hartland Plastics Co. c. mid-1950s. BOXED $350, LOOSE $175

Broken Arrow

A western TV drama patterned after the book of same title by Elliott Arnold and the ensuing motion picture of 1950 starring James Stewart and Jeff Chandler. The TV series starred Michael Ansara as Cochise, chief of the Apaches, and John Lupton as Tom Jeffords, an Indian agent. The two developed a trusting "blood brother" relationship to correct injustices caused either by whites or Indians. The series began September 25, 1956 on ABC-TV and continued through September 23, 1958 before syndication under *Cochise* title.

1
"MICHAEL ANSARA AS COCHISE" 3.25x5.25″ bw photo card c. late 1950s. $5

2
"BROKEN ARROW/COCHISE" 9x9.5x3″ boxed figure with accessories by Hartland Plastics Co. c. 1957-1958. BOXED $200, LOOSE $125

3
"JOHN LUPTON AS TOM JEF-FORDS" 8x10″ school tablet with color cover c. 1957. $20

4
"BROKEN ARROW/TOM JEF-FORDS" 9x9.5x3″ boxed figure with accessories by Hartland Plastics Co. c. 1957. BOXED $400, LOOSE $250

5
"MICHAEL ANSARA" auto-graphed 5x7″ bw photo c. late 1950s. $50

6
"BROKEN ARROW" 7x7.25″ color envelope holding theme music 45 rpm RCA Victor record c. 1957. $30

7
"BROKEN ARROW" 6.5x8″ first edition Simon & Schuster Little Golden Book © 1957. $12

8
"BROKEN ARROW" boxed set of four 11x13.5″ "Sta-N-Place" frame tray inlay color jigsaw puzzles c. 1957. BOXED $75, EACH $15

1

2

3

4

5

6

7

8

Buck Jones (1889–1942)

Born Charles Gebhart in Vincennes, Indiana, November 12, 1889, the family moved in 1901 to Oklahoma cattle ranching. His cowpunching experience on the ranch was followed by experiences as an Indianapolis raceway mechanic, Army service in the Philippines and Mexican Border War, trick rider for the 101 Ranch Wild West Show and, briefly, Ringling Bros. Circus.

Jones' first movie experiences were as stuntman for early two-reelers beginning about 1917. His first starring role was in a 1920 film titled *The Last Straw*. His association with Fox Studios lasted eight years and was highly successful for both. There was no success to his independent attempts, after leaving Fox, to become a filmmaker. Equally disastrous was his Buck Jones Wild West Show that folded financially after about one month on the road. He returned to studio filming to begin the 1930s.

His first film under contract to Beverly Pictures, *The Lone Rider,* released by Columbia in 1930, was also his first talking movie. Acceptance was enthusiastic and more successful films followed via Columbia through 1934. He again formed his own picture company for films to be released by Universal over the next three years. A dispute with Universal returned him to Columbia in 1937–1938.

1937 also began his brief 39-episode *Hoofbeats* radio show sponsored by Grape-Nuts Flakes. The adventures of Buck and his horse Silver were narrated by an anonymous "Old Wrangler" who also urged cereal consumption to obtain *Buck Jones Rangers Club* premiums, although a similar club had existed from almost a decade earlier.

His final movie days were in the early 1940s "Rough Riders" series of Monogram Pictures, also featuring Tim McCoy and Raymond Hatton. His career totaled more than 125 movies. His final starring role was in *Dawn of the Great Divide* released December 18, 1942—less than a month after his November 30 untimely death due to fire that swept through Boston's famous Coconut Grove nightclub.

BUCK JONES
Star in Fox Productions

1

2

3

6

4

5

1
BUCK JONES 2x3.25″ bw card from "Stars Of The Movie World" 80-card set by American Caramel Co. 1920s. $10

2
BUCK JONES 3.25x5.25″ monochrome exhibit card 1930s. $8

3
BUCK JONES 18x25″ color felt movie banner 1930s. $200

4
"CHARLES JONES" 27x41″ poster for film "Snowdrift" before 'Buck' nickname 1923. $300

5
"THE ROUGH RIDERS" 27x41″ movie poster for "Arizona Bound" 1941. $125

6
"BUCK JONES IN THE RED RIDER" 4.5x6″ cardboard pop gun for 1934 serial. $75

7
''BUCK JONES'' 36″ air rifle
1930s. $100

8
''HIDDEN VALLEY'' 9x12″
sheet music © 1936. $35

9
BUCK JONES 37″ tall pressed
wood guitar 1930s. $150

10
''SONGS OF THE WESTERN
TRAILS'' 9x12″ photo and music
folio © 1940. $35

11
''BUCK JONES AND SILVER''
16.5x17.25″ brown/purple/white
bandanna c. 1930s. $150

12
''BEST WISHES/BUCK JONES
& SILVER'' 5x7″ bw photo late
1930s. $20

13
''BUCK JONES IN THE FIGHT-
ING CODE'' 4.75x5.25″ Whitman
Big Little Book © 1934. $40

14
''BUCK JONES IN RIDE 'EM
COWBOY'' 3.5x4.5″ Whitman
Big Little Book © 1937. $35

15
''THE ROUGH RIDERS''
3.5x4.5″ Whitman Better Little
Book © 1943. $30

16
''A TIMELY ARRIVAL'' 2.5x3″
booklet from series by Goudey
Gum © 1934. EACH $40

17
''ON THE SIX-GUN TRAIL''
2.5x3.75″ Whitman booklet
© 1939. $20

18
''COWBOY MASQUERADE''
3.5x3.5″ Whitman booklet from
''Buddy Book'' series © 1938.
$35

7

8

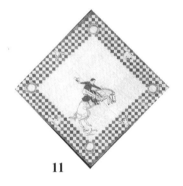

9

10

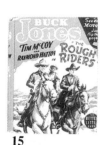

11

12

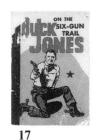

13

14

15

16

17

18

19

20

21

22

23

24

25

26

27

28

29

30

19
BUCK JONES 7x10″ Vol. 1 #3
Dell pulp magazine for September
1937. $35

20
''BUCK JONES'' 7.5x10″ issue
#2 of Dell comic book for April-
June 1951. $20

21
''BUCK JONES ANNUAL''
7.25x9.5″ English comic strip
book 1957. $25

22
''BUCK JONES'' 2.25x3″ card
#167 from Buck Jones series
numbered 162-193 in total set of
224 Whitman cards published
1937. EACH $20

23
''BUCK JONES'' 2.75″ Dixie Ice
Cream cup lid 1941. $25

24
''BUCK JONES'' 8x10″ Dixie Ice
Cream picture 1941. $35

25
''BUCK JONES'' 4.25x5.75″
''Movie Book'' offered as Daisy
air rifle premium c. 1938. $50

26
''BUCK JONES'' 3.5x6.25″ premium folder by Grape-Nuts Flakes
1937. $60

27
BUCK JONES 9x12″ song folio c.
1932. $35

28
''RANGER'' 1.75″ tall metal club
badge c. 1937. $75

29
''RANGERS CLUB OF AMER-
ICA'' 8.5″ long leather holster
1930s. $150

30
''YOUR PAL BUCK JONES''
8x10″ photo 1930s. $35

Buffalo Bill, Jr.

A brief Saturday morning TV series of 40 episodes syndicated in 1955. Starring in the title role was Dick Jones as an orphan adopted by Judge Ben Wiley and later named Marshal of Wileyville, Texas. Supporting stars were Nancy Gilbert as Calamity, Bill's younger sister, and Harry Cheshire as the Judge. The series was produced and syndicated by Gene Autry Flying A Productions.

1
"DICK JONES/BUFFALO BILL JR." 4x5" bw photo with facsimile signature c. 1955. $20

2
"BUFFALO BILL JR." 13x16" sales promotion kit folder by CBS-TV Film Sales for syndication c. late 1950s. $35

3
"BUFFALO BILL JR." 7.5x10" Dell comic book #7 for February-April 1958. $10

4
"BUFFALO BILL JR." 7.5x10" Gold Key comic book issue #1 for June 1965. $7

5
"BUFFALO BILL JR." 11x13.5" frame tray inlay jigsaw puzzle picturing him with Nancy Gilbert as Calamity, his younger sister, © 1956. $20

6
"BUFFALO BILL JR." 11x13.5" frame tray inlay jigsaw puzzle © 1956. $20

7
"BUFFALO BILL JR." 6.5x8x2" deep boxed jigsaw puzzle with same scene as #5 © 1956. $20

8
"BUFFALO BILL JR." child's two-part cowboy outfit of flannel trimmed by plastic fringe plus simulated fur c. late 1950s. $75

1

2

3

4

5

6

7

8

Charles Starrett (1904–1986)

A tall, muscular, athletic western star best remembered for 65 Durango Kid films, although also a very competent and prolific cowboy star credited with the longest association to a single studio (Columbia) through the full course of his 1935–1952 acting career. Starrett was not born to the saddle as were several of his peers. Rather, his youth and early years were spent in military school followed by Dartmouth College and then skipping from play-writing for Wanamaker's department store to actual stock company performances. His first actual movie and others to follow were not of western nature, although a reputation was built as a very effective Royal Mountie portrayer. His western films began in 1935 and the Durango Kid series followed in 1940 to continue until his 1952 retirement from acting. As Durango, his trademark was the black outfit and matching triangular mask over his lower face. He retired in 1952, still at the height of his popularity after a career of 131 western films.

1

2

3

4

5

6

7

8

9

10

11

1
"CHARLES 'DURANGO' STARRETT" autographed 8x10″ bw glossy photo c. late 1940s. $50

2
"GRIT STORY SECTION" 8.5x11.5″ supplement to January 8, 1939 newspaper. $20

3
"CHARLES STARRETT" 2.75″ Dixie Ice Cream lid 1940. $20

4
"CHARLES STARRETT" 8x10″ Dixie Ice Cream picture 1937. $35

5
"CHARLES STARRETT" 8x10″ Dixie Ice Cream picture 1940. $30

6
"CHARLES STARRETT" 8x10″ Dixie Ice Cream picture 1942. $25

7
"CHARLES STARRETT" 8x10″ Dixie Ice Cream picture 1940s. $25

8
"THE BLAZING TRAIL" 11x14″ lobby card 1949. $15

9
"THE DURANGO KID" 7.5x10″ Vol. 1 #3 comic book by Magazine Enterprises for February-March 1950. $65

10
"THE DURANGO KID" 7.5x10″ Vol. 1 #4 comic book by Magazine Enterprises for April-May 1950. $65

11
"BANDITS OF EL DORADO" 27x41″ movie poster 1949. $50

Cheyenne

An oft-used geographic name in western film lore, Cheyenne became the personal name for the star of the Warner Bros. TV series beginning September 20, 1955. The series starred massive Clint Walker as Cheyenne Bodie, a roving loner throughout the west following the Civil War. A precedent for the series could be considered a film of 10 years earlier, *Song of Old Wyoming*, casting Al LaRue as a similar reclusive "Cheyenne Kid" gunfighter. Walker left the TV series in 1958 although it continued under the same title starring Ty Hardin as Bronco Lane. Walker returned to the role in 1959 until the final telecast on September 13, 1963.

1
"ACME BOOTS" 8.5x14.75" diecut rigid color cardboard store sign with easel back c. 1957. $175

2
"TV GUIDE" 5x7.5" issue for August 31, 1957. $25

3
"TV GUIDE" 5x7.5" issue for November 21, 1959. $25

4
"CLINT WALKER" 3.5x5.5" Warner Bros. color photo fan card c. 1960. $25

5
AUTOGRAPHED "CLINT WALKER" 8x10" glossy bw photo c. 1960. $60

6
"CLINT WALKER" 3.5x5.5" sepia postcard from English "Picturegoer" series c. 1960. $20

7
"TV'S CHEYENNE" 17x24x2.5" boxed Target Game English made by Mettoy © 1962. BOXED $300, LOOSE $150

8
"CHEYENNE" 32x5x2" boxed "Singin' Saddle Gun" by Daisy Mfg. Co. © 1959. BOXED $150, LOOSE $75

9
"CHEYENNE" 12x14x3" boxed leather double holster and metal cap gun set by Daisy Mfg. Co. © 1959. BOXED $300, LOOSE $150

1

2

3

4

5

6

7

8

9

10

11

12

13

14

15

16

17

18

19

20

21

22

23

10
CHEYENNE 9″ tall replica figure by Hartland Plastics Co. c. 1960. BOXED (NOT SHOWN) $250, LOOSE $125

11
CHEYENNE 5.5x7.5″ Whitman book #1587 © 1958. $20

12
CHEYENNE 8.5x11″ Whitman coloring book #1169 © 1958. $35

13
CHEYENNE 7.25x10″ English ''Comic Album'' © 1957. $40

14
CHEYENNE 7.5x10.5″ English ''T.V. Bumper Book'' © 1958. $40

15
''CHEYENNE ANNUAL'' 7.25x10″ English book © 1961. $35

16
''CHEYENNE ANNUAL'' 7.25x10″ English book © 1961. $35

17
CHEYENNE 10x14″ frame tray inlay jigsaw puzzle by Milton Bradley © 1957. $25

18
CHEYENNE 6.5x10x1″ boxed board game by Milton Bradley © 1957. $60

19
CHEYENNE 9.5x19x2″ boxed board game with Clint Walker art © 1958. $70

20
CHEYENNE 9.5x19x2″ boxed Milton Bradley board game with Ty Hardin art © 1959. $60

21
CHEYENNE 8x10″ school tablet with color cover c. 1958. $20

22
CHEYENNE 45 rpm RCA Victor record c. late 1950s. $40

23
CHEYENNE 28″ long fabric trousers c. 1960. $40

The Cisco Kid

The Cisco Kid is certainly no longer a "kid" in terms of age. Originally created in the first decade of the 1900s by writer O. Henry (Sydney Porter), Cisco came to film life in the 1929 Fox film *In Old Arizona* starring Warner Baxter as Cisco. The role earned Baxter a Western Oscar and the film itself earned four others. Baxter again appeared in the 1931 Fox sequel *The Cisco Kid*. Later movie versions came in 1939 (*The Cisco Kid And The Lady,* starring Cesar Romero, 20th Century Fox) and 1945 (*The Cisco Kid Returns,* starring Duncan Renaldo, Monogram Pictures). Renaldo went on to portray Cisco in the immensely popular early 1950s TV series, aided by sidekick Pancho (Leo Carillo). A total 156 episodes were produced by ZIV Television (all in forerunner color as the nation's TV sets were limited to black-and-white films) for original distribution years of 1950–1956.

1
"CESAR ROMERO" 3.5x5.5" tinted sepia English postcard for movie "Lucky Cisco Kid" of 1940. $15

2
"LUCKY CISCO KID" 27x41" poster, 1940. $175

3
"SOUTH OF THE RIO GRANDE" 27x41" poster, 1945. $150

4
"BEAUTY AND THE BANDIT" 27x41" poster, 1946. $125

5
"IN OLD NEW MEXICO" 9.5x12" paper handbill for Cisco Kid film of 1945. $15

6
"ROBIN HOOD OF MONTE-REY" 7x9.5" paper handbill for Cisco Kid film of 1947. $15

7
CISCO KID & PANCHO 3.5x5.5" postcard for Tip-Top Bread c. 1953. $20

8
CISCO KID & DIABLO 8x10" bw photo c. 1953. $25

9
CISCO KID & DIABLO 8x10" bw Butternut Bread photo 1956. $30

10
"RODEO" 9x25" felt pennant c. early 1950s. $40

11
"POLICE CIRCUS" 4x18" bumper sticker c. early 1950s. $25

1

2   3

4

5   6

7   8   9

10   11

12

13

14

15

16

17

18

19

20

21

12
CISCO KID 4x9x1.5″ boxed 9″ cap gun by Lone Star c. early 1950s. BOXED $150, LOOSE $75

13
CISCO KID 13x13.5x2″ boxed leather double holster set c. early 1950s. BOXED $150, LOOSE $50

14
CISCO KID 40″ tall stick horse toy with padded vinyl head c. early 1950s. $60

15
CISCO KID & PANCHO 11x14″ Saalfield coloring book © 1951. $35

16
CISCO KID 11x14″ Doubleday coloring book © 1953. $30

17
CISCO KID 4x4.5x1″ boxed crayon set c. early 1950s. $25

18
CISCO KID 11x14″ Saalfield coloring book © 1954. $35

19
CISCO KID 11x12.5″ Saalfield coloring book c. early 1950s. $35

20
CISCO KID 7x10″ English "Comic Album" © 1953. $25

21
CISCO KID 16x16.5″ opened album sheet for mounting end labels from Tip-Top Bread. Example photo shows both sides of sheet and folded front cover c. 1953. $100

22
CISCO KID & PANCHO 3x3″ portrait end labels from Tip-Top Bread c. 1952. EACH $8

23
CISCO KID & PANCHO 3x3″ action scene end labels from Tip-Top Bread c. 1952. EACH $8

24
CISCO KID 10x18″ paper sign for imprinting name of local television sponsor c. 1952. $125

25
CISCO KID 9x12″ folder holding publicity and promotion materials from ZIV Television c. 1950-1951. $150

26
CISCO KID 2.5x4″ card holding crepe paper ''Humming Lariat'' c. early 1950s. $85

27
CISCO KID 3.25x4.25″ card of five plastic clothing buttons c. 1951. $30

28
''CISCO KID AMIGOS'' 5x7.5″ envelope holding club member materials sponsored by Donald Duck Bread of Durkee Baking Co. c. 1950. $75

29
CISCO KID 10x11.5x2″ boxed set of two Saalfield jigsaw puzzles © 1951. $50

30
CISCO KID & PANCHO 2.5″ tall by 5″ dia. white glass cereal bowl c. early 1950s. $35

31
CISCO KID 10.5x12.5″ stiff paper mask with local TV sponsor imprint on back © 1949. $25

32
PANCHO 10.5x12.5″ companion paper mask to #31. $25

22

23

24

25

26

27

28

29

30

31   **32**

Colt .45

A Warner Bros. TV series based loosely on the direct descendants of the 19th century Samuel Colt firearms family. The TV series featured Christopher Colt as a sales representative for firearms but in actuality a government agent tracking outlaws during the U.S. Grant presidency. A replica Colt .45 Peacemaker Rifle was obviously his chosen weapon. Wayde Preston starred as Christopher Colt and Donald May portrayed his cousin Sam Colt, Jr. A total 67 episodes were produced during the October 18, 1957 to September 20, 1960 series run.

1

1
"CHRIS COLT" 9″ tall boxed Hartland Plastics Co. replica figure © 1958. BOXED $300, LOOSE $175

2
"WAYDE PRESTON" 3.5x5.5″ Warner Bros. color postcard c. 1959. $15

3
"COLT .45" 8x10.5″ Saalfield coloring book © 1959. $30

4
"WAYDE PRESTON" 8x10″ school tablet with color cover c. 1959. $25

5
"WAYDE PRESTON" 3.5x5.5″ bw fan postcard c. 1960. $15

2

3

4

5

Dale Evans (b. 1912)

The proclaimed "Queen of the West" due to her roles in cowboy films, principally with her husband, Roy Rogers. Born Frances Smith, she was a frequent radio songstress in the late 1930s and early 1940s including regular appearances on the *Edgar Bergen & Charlie McCarthy Show* and later the *Jack Carson Show*. Her first appearance in a Roy Rogers film came in the 1944 release *The Cowboy And The Senorita*. She wed widower Rogers December 31, 1947 and thereafter appeared with him in more than 25 films. Later years have been devoted to spiritual and inspirational writings and appearances.

1
DALE EVANS 9.25x12″ sheet music © 1939. $30

2
"RADIO HIT SONGS" 9x12″ song folio © 1943. $25

3
"WESTERN SONGS" 10x12.5″ folio © 1947. $35

4
"BARN DANCE" 8.5x10.5″ magazine © January 1948. $40

5
"DALE EVANS" 8x10″ color Dixie Ice Cream picture c. 1945. $50

6
"DALE EVANS" 8x10″ color Dixie Ice Cream picture c. 1945. $30

7
"DALE EVANS" 3.5x5.5″ sepia card #W291 from English "Picturegoer" series c. 1940s. $20

8
"DALE EVANS" 7.5x10″ DC comic book #5 for May-June 1949. $65

9
"DALE EVANS" 7.5x10″ DC comic book #7 for September-October 1949. $65

10
"DALE EVANS" 7.5x10″ Dell comic book #10 for January-March 1956. $20

11
"DALE EVANS" 3.5x5.5″ monochrome exhibit card c. 1950. $15

12
AUTOGRAPHED "DALE EVANS" 8x10″ color photo c. 1950s. $30

1

2

3

4

5

6

7

8

9

10

11

12

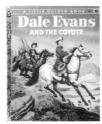

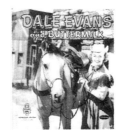

13　　　　**14**　　　　**15**

16　　　　**17**　　　　**18**

19

20

21

22

23

24　　　　**25**

13
DALE EVANS 11x14″ Whitman coloring book © 1957. $40

14
DALE EVANS 6.75x8″ Little Golden Book © 1956. $15

15
DALE EVANS 5.5x6.5″ Whitman book co-featuring her horse Buttermilk © 1956. $20

16
DALE EVANS 5.5x7.75″ Whitman novel © 1958. $20

17
"TO MY SON" 6x8.5″ book of letters written by her to son Tom © 1957. $20

18
"SALUTE TO SANDY" 5.5x7.5″ commemorative book for death of son Sandy in military service © 1967. $15

19
"CHRISTMAS IS ALWAYS" 4.5x6.5″ inspirational holiday book © 1963. $15

20
DALE-ROY 6.5x7.5″ paper album holding 78 rpm inspirational Little Golden Record c. mid-1950s. $25

21
"IT'S REAL" 12.25x12.25″ cardboard album holding 33 1/3 rpm record of sacred songs c. 1970s. $20

22
DALE EVANS 3.75x5″ envelope holding color water transfer decal picture c. 1950. $30

23
DALE EVANS 4.5x4.5″ packet of View-Master reel set c. 1956. $40

24
DALE & BULLET 8x10″ school tablet with color cover c. 1956. $30

25
DALE & BULLET 4x5″ frame tray inlay jigsaw puzzle © 1956. $20

26
DALE EVANS 11x13x2″ boxed
set of leather holsters and metal
cap guns c. 1950s. BOXED $400,
LOOSE $200

27
''DALE EVANS'' set of 8″ long
metal cap guns and leather holsters c. 1950s. $150

28
DALE EVANS 11x14x2″ boxed
felt and corduroy vest and skirt
cowgirl outfit c. late 1940s. $200

29
DALE EVANS size 14/32 young
girl's T-shirt c. 1950s. $75

30
DALE EVANS & BUTTERMILK
8″ tall Hartland Plastics Co. replica figure c. 1950s. BOXED
(NOT SHOWN) $300, LOOSE
$125

31
DALE EVANS 7x8″ terrycloth
bath mitt c. mid-1950s. $35

32
DALE EVANS 7.5x9″ fabric covered plastic school bag c. 1950.
$100

33
DALE EVANS size 3 child's felt
slippers c. mid-1950s. $85

34
DALE EVANS black felt hat with
bw hatband also inscribed ''Queen
Of The West'' c. 1950. $50

35
DALE EVANS 3.5x5.5x3″ deep
display box holding wristwatch by
Ingraham c. 1951. BOXED $250,
LOOSE $75

26

27

28

29

31

32

30

33

35

34

Daniel Boone

A well-done fictionalized TV series about the life and accomplishments of the late 18th century folk hero, his family and sidekicks. The series starred Fess Parker throughout its original six-year run. Parker had earlier successfully portrayed a similar folk hero (see Davy Crockett-Disney). Among the many featured stars of the Boone series were Patricia Blair (wife Rebecca), Ed Ames (Mingo), Jimmy Dean (Gosh Clements), Roosevelt Grier (Gabe Cooper) plus numerous well-known guest stars. The series began September 24, 1964 and concluded August 27, 1970 after 165 episodes.

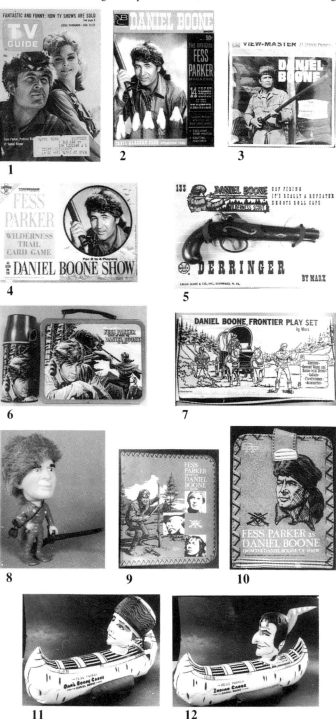

1
TV GUIDE 5x7.5″ issue for week of August 21, 1965. $10

2
DANIEL BOONE 8.5x11″ Vol. 1 #1 magazine © 1965. $25

3
DANIEL BOONE 4.5x4.5″ packet View-Master reel set © 1965. $25

4
TRANSOGRAM CARD GAME 7x10x2″ © 1964. $30

5
DERRINGER CAP PISTOL by Marx c. 1965. CARDED $50, LOOSE $25

6
STEEL LUNCH BOX and 6.5″ bottle by King-Seeley Co. c. 1965. BOX $125, BOTTLE $75

7
DANIEL BOONE 4x13x24″ ''Frontier Play Set'' of 5″ tall plastic figures and accessories by Marx Toys c. 1965. $200

8
''FESS PARKER AS DANIEL BOONE'' 5.25″ tall plastic figure © 1964. COMPLETE $125, FIGURE ONLY $35

9
DANIEL BOONE 10x12″ vinyl over rigid cardboard three-ring school notebook © 1964. $30

10
DANIEL BOONE 3.5x4.5″ vinyl billfold including interior photos from TV series © 1964. $30

11
''DAN'L BOONE CANOE'' 5x10x17″ long inflated vinyl toy © 1965. $35

12
''INDIAN CANOE'' companion toy to #11 © 1965. $25

Davy Crockett (Disney)

A mid-1950s phenomenally successful folk hero characterization stemming from mini-series versions telecast on the early Disneyland series. Fess Parker starred as the coonskin-capped adventurer in five biography segments between December 15, 1954 to December 14, 1955 titled *Davy Crockett, Indian Fighter; Davy Crockett Goes To Congress, Davy Crockett At The Alamo, Davy Crockett's Keelboat Race, Davy Crockett And The River Pirates.* Full length theater films released by Buena Vista productions of Disney Studios, both starring Parker, were *Davy Crockett, King Of The Wild Frontier* (1955) and *Davy Crockett And The River Pirates* (1956). The Crockett popularity unleashed hundreds of merchandise items.

1
TV GUIDE 5x7.5″ issue for week of April 30, 1955. $30

2
DELL 8.5x11″ Vol. 1 #1, 1955 magazine. $35

3
CROCKETT 8.5x11″ Whitman coloring book © 1955. $45

4
DAVY CROCKETT 6x7.75″ Whitman book © 1955. $25

5
DAVY CROCKETT 8.5x11″ Big Golden Book © 1955. $25

6
DAVY CROCKETT 8.5x11″ Simon & Schuster book with 48 stamps © 1955. UNUSED $50, STAMPS MOUNTED $25

7
DAVY CROCKETT-MIKE FINK 8.5x11″ Simon & Schuster book © 1955. $30

8
DAVY CROCKETT 6.5x8″ Simon & Schuster book © 1955. $30

9
DAVY CROCKETT 7.5x10″ Dell comic book #639 from 1955. $20

10
DAVY CROCKETT 7.5x10″ Dell comic book #671 from 1955. $20

11
''CANDIES AND TOY'' box 2.5×4″with cut-out c. 1956. $40

12
DAVY CROCKETT 2.75x3.75″ card by Topps gum © 1956. ORANGE BACK #1-80 EACH $3, GREEN BACK #1A-80A EACH $4

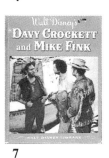

1

2

3

4

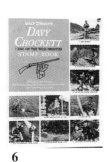

5

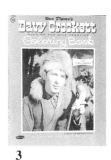

6

7

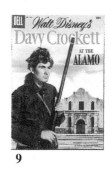

8

9

10

11

12

13   **14**

15   **16**

17   **18**

19

20

21

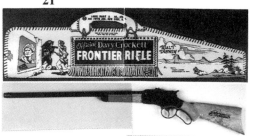

22

13
"DAVY CROCKETT ADVEN-
TURES" 10x13x2" boxed board
game c. 1955. $60

14
DAVY CROCKETT "INDIAN
SCOUTING" 14.5x19x2" boxed
Whitman game © 1955. $75

15
DAVY CROCKETT "FRON-
TIERLAND" 8x16x2" boxed Par-
ker Brothers game c. 1955. $40

16
DAVY CROCKETT "RESCUE
RACE" 10x19.5x2" boxed Ga-
briel Toys game © 1955. $50

17
DAVY CROCKETT 10.5x14.5"
lithographed tin tray c. 1955. $75

18
DAVY CROCKETT 12.5x17" lithographed tin tray c. 1955. $100

19
DAVY CROCKETT 6.5x8.5x4"
deep steel lunch box by Adco-Liberty Co. 1955. $175

20
DAVY CROCKETT-KIT CAR-
SON 6.5x8.5x4" deep steel lunch
box by Adco-Liberty Co. 1955.
BOX $185, BOTTLE (NOT
SHOWN) $60

21
DAVY CROCKETT 25" long
plastic and silvered metal "Buffalo Rifle" cap-firing replica by
Hubley Toys c. mid-1950s. $150

22
DAVY CROCKETT 32" long cap-
firing "Frontier Rifle" replica
with carrying case by Marx Toys
c. 1955. BOXED $150, LOOSE
$75

23
DAVY CROCKETT "FRON-
TIERLAND" 12.5x22.5x4.5"
boxed "Hunter Outfit" of belt and
buckle, replica powder horn and
24" long "Buffalo Rifle" plus
simulated coonskin cap by Eddy
Mfg. Co. c. 1955. $400

23

24
DAVY CROCKETT "FRON-
TIERLAND" 14.5x14.5x4" deep
boxed outfit of holster belt and
metal cap pistol, replica powder
horn, simulated coonskin cap c.
1955. $200

24

25
DAVY CROCKETT 2x2x7.5"
boxed 7" plastic replica powder
horn with carrying cord c. 1955.
BOXED $75, LOOSE $40

25

26

26
DAVY CROCKETT "FRON-
TIERLAND" 5x8" vinyl holster
holding clear plastic gun-shaped
pencil case c. 1956. $75

27
DAVY CROCKETT 3x6.5x9"
wide box holding 6" long metal
projection gun and four bw films
for it by Stephens Products Co. c.
mid-1950s. BOXED $125,
LOOSE $75

27

28
DAVY CROCKETT 10.5x13x1.5"
deep boxed girl's vinyl and fabric
playsuit including simulated fur
cap by Ben Cooper Co. c. 1955.
BOXED $125, LOOSE $60

29
DAVY CROCKETT fabric jeans
with vinyl fringe plus leather
picture patch on back pockets by
Blue Bell Co. c. mid-1950s. $60

28   **29**

30
DAVY CROCKETT 2.5x2.5x6"
tall boxed wood and plastic
jointed push puppet figure by
Kohner Bros. c. 1956. BOXED
$125, LOOSE $60

31
DAVY CROCKETT 1.25x3.25"
tall enameled metal pocket flashlight by Bantam Lite Co. c. mid-
1950s. $30

30   **31**

32

33

34

35

36

37

38

39

40

41

32
DAVY CROCKETT 2″ tall hard plastic figure from Marx Toys Co. playset c. 1955. $25

33
"DAVY CROCKETT AT THE ALAMO" 14x23x4″ boxed Marx Toys playset #3544 c. 1955. $800

34
"DAVY CROCKETT AT THE ALAMO" 11x23x3″ boxed Marx Toys playset c. mid-1950s. $600

35
DAVY CROCKETT 12″ tall canister holding parts for assembly of Alamo model of plastic and clay by Practi-Cole Products c. 1955. $125

36
DAVY CROCKETT 17x17x13″ tall vinyl covered TV seat with removable lid for storage c. mid-1950s. $250

37
DAVY CROCKETT 4x5x1″ boxed brown vinyl wallet with color art front and back c. 1955. BOXED $75, LOOSE $40

38
DAVY CROCKETT 4.5x8.5″ card holding stainless steel "Chow Set" spoon and fork c. 1956. CARDED $65, LOOSE $25

39
DAVY CROCKETT 10x12x6″ deep stiff cardboard suitcase with plastic handle and brass hinges by Neevel Co. c. mid-1950s. $50

40
DAVY CROCKETT 7x7.5″ paper album holding Little Golden Record c. 1955. $15

41
DAVY CROCKETT 3x3.5x7.5″ wide display box holding wristwatch positioned on replica powder horn c. 1955. BOXED $350, WATCH ONLY $100

TOM MIX

"Tom Mix and Tony," child's wooden riding toy by The Mengel Co., 1930s, **$350.**

All of the following items, except "Miracle Riders" booklet, are premiums from Ralston-Purina Co. Leather and cloth vest with rwb cloth patch, 1935, **$250**; leather wrist cuffs with Straight Shooters logo, 1935, **$250**; leather and cloth chaps with rwb cloth patch, 1935, **$350**; leather holster with Straight Shooters logo, 1935, **$300**; "Ralston Straight Shooters" wooden gun with barrel that opens and cylinder that spins, 1933, **$150**; "Tom Mix" wooden gun with cardboard labels on grips and no moving parts, 1939, **$125**; Lasso of rwb twine with "Tom Mix Eats Ralston . . ." endorsement on wooden handle, 1933, **$125**; "Tom Mix Miracle Riders," Tootsie Pop premium album holding complete set of 15 numbered photos from the movie serial by Mascot Pictures, 1935, **$500**; "Tom Mix Western Movie" (front and back shown) cardboard boxes holding two different bw paper films on wooden rollers with scenes from *Rustler's Roundup* and *The Miracle Rider*, 1935, each **$175.**

GENE AUTRY

"Gene Autry Cowboy Paint Book" by Merrill Publishing Co., 1940, **$40**; "The Gene Autry Jump-Up Book" by Adprint Limited London, 1955, **$75**; "Gene Autry's Cowboy Songs and Mountain Ballads" by M.M. Cole Publishing Co., 1932, **$35**; "Gene Autry in Public Cowboy No. 1" by Whitman Publishing Co., 1938, **$35**; "Gene Autry in Person" press book binder cover and 40 pages of text and photos to promote his winter personal appearance tour, 1936, **$200**; "Always Your Pal Gene Autry" 9" glazed china dinner plate from five-piece setting by Knowles, 1950, **$100**; "Gene Autry" horseshoe nail ring on original card by Albin Enterprises, c. 1950, **$175.**

"Gene Autry" rubber boots by Servus Rubber Co., 1950s, **$150**; Gene Autry 8" tall glazed ceramic figure on horseshoe shaped base, 1950s, **$400**; "Gene Autry Official Ranch Outfit" with leather and metal double holsters and two "Gene Autry" cap guns by Leslie-Henry Co., 1950s, **$600**; "Gene Autry Official Cowboy Spurs" with original box by Leslie-Henry, Inc., 1950s, **$100.**

THE LONE RANGER

"The Lone Ranger Target," lithographed tin, 9 1/2" square version by Marx Toys, 1930s, **$50**; "The Lone Ranger Chuck Wagon Lantern," kerosene-fueled, made of metal and glass, original box, R.E. Dietz Co., 1950s, **$300**; "The Lone Ranger" action (mechanical) bank, plastic, E.J. Kahn & Co., late 1940s, **$300**; "Tonto Indian Outfit" with "Tonto" headdress and belt, unmarked holster, and "Tex" gun by Hubley, original box by esquire novelty co., 1950s, **$400.**

"Lone-Ranger Hi-Yo Silver" cast-iron cap gun by Kilgore, 1930s, **$150**; "The Lone Ranger Flashlight Pistol" and box, battery operated light bulb in barrel end of plastic gun with metal trigger and hammer, Marx Toys, 1950s, **$250**; "The Lone Ranger Coloring Book" by Whitman Publishing Co., 1954, **$60**; "The Lone Ranger Picture Puzzle," frame-tray style by Whitman Publishing Co., 1953, **$25**; "The Lone Ranger Official Billfold," leather zippered wallet with identification card matching box art by Hidecraft, 1947, **$150**; "Chief Scout," set of five postal mailing cards awarded to Silvercup Bread club members as they advanced from First Degree Scout to Fifth Degree Scout, whereupon member became a Chief Lone Ranger Safety Scout and was awarded a Chief Scout Badge, mid 1930s, set **$375**; *The Lone Ranger and Dead Men's Mine*, Better Little Book #1407 by Whitman Publishing Co., 1939, **$40.**

ROY ROGERS

"Roy Rogers Rodeo" metal lamp and parchment shade by Pearson Industries, inner revolving drum shows nine pictures of Roy and Trigger. Outer shade with acutal rodeo photos, 1949. Outer shade with artwork rodeo scenes, 1950. Either version, **$1,000**; "Dale Evans" plaster lamp with generic western scenes on parchment shade by Plasto Mfg. Co., 1950s, **$250**; "Roy Rogers" lithographed tin hauler and van trailer with Nellybelle Jeep (plastic) and plastic figures of Roy, Dale, Bullet, Pat Brady, and two horses by Marx Toys, 1950s, **$250**; Roy Rogers and Trigger plastic figure with saddle, hat, and two guns by Hartland Plastics, 1960s, **$150**; "Roy Rogers and Dale Evans Double R Bar Ranch" vacuum bottle by The American Thermos Bottle Co., 1955, **$60**; "Roy Rogers Trigger Savings Bank" of lithographed tin to be wall mounted, The Ohio Art Co., 1950s, **$150**; "Roy Rogers Dale Evans Chow Wagon" steel-domed lunch box by The American Thermos Products Co., 1955, **$150.**

"Roy Rogers Rodeo" stiff cardboard sign for Madison Square Garden event, 1950s, **$400**; "The Roy Rogers Show" announcement folder holding 8 x 10" glossy photo of Roy holding floor model "Mutual" radio microphone as he sits on Trigger to promote debut of radio show, 1944, **$200**; "The Double-R-Bar Ranch News" fan club magazine, October, 1943, **$150**; "Dale Evans Queen of the West Wrist Watch" in original box by Ingraham, 1949, **$300**; "Lore of the West," 78 rpm RCA Victor record and illustrated story album, 1949, **$100**; "Roy Rogers' pal Pat Brady Coloring Book" by Whitman Publishing Co., 1955, **$35.**

HOPALONG CASSIDY

Hopalong Cassidy, 13 1/2" plaster carnival statue, unmarked, c. 1950, **$400**; "Hopalong Cassidy Official Bar 20 T-V Chair," 22" tall, canvas-on-wood frame that folds, c. 1950, **$500**; "Hopalong Cassidy" glass lamp with parchment shade by Aladdin, c. 1950, **$400**; "Hopalong Cassidy's Target Game," lithographed tin by Marx Toys, c. 1950, **$250**; "Hopalong Cassidy Bar-20 Ranch" plastic lamp with revolving inner cylinder depicting Hoppy and stage-coach by Econolite Corp., c. 1950, **$400.**

"Hopalong Cassidy" vacuum bottle by Aladdin Industries, Inc., 1954, **$90**; "Hopalong Cassidy" lunch box by Aladdin Industries, Inc., 1954, **$250**; "Hopalong Cassidy Pistol and Spurs" in box, All Metal Products Co., c. 1950, **$500**; "Hopalong Cassidy Holster Set," double guns and leather holsters in box, All Metal Products Co., c. 1950, **$800**; "Hoppy's Favorite Milk Lakeside Dairy," half gallon glass bottle, c. 1950, **$150.**

1950S WESTERN STARS

"Straight Arrow Target Game," lithographed tin target with wood and spring steel crossbow to shoot small magnetic disk tipped with feathers, Novel Novelties, Inc., c. 1949, **$150**; Davy Crockett, 15 1/2" tall plaster carnival statue, c. 1955, **$100**; "Laramie Cowboy Holster Set," double holsters and belt plus cap guns (in this example) marked "Cisco Kid," Clarke Bros. (Liverpool) Ltd., 1960, **$250**; "Brave Eagle" lunch box by American Thermos Bottle Co., c. 1955, **$200**.

"Wild Bill Hickok and Jingles Poney Express Game" by Built-Rite, 1956, **$40**; "Lash LaRue Western" comic book No. 25, Fawcett Publications, Inc., February, 1952, **$12**; "Annie Oakley Cut-Out Dolls," uncut in folder, Watkins-Strathmore, 1956, **$50**; "Zorro/Seven-Up," easel-back stiff cardboard store sign, 1957, **$200**; "Duncan Renaldo 'The TV Cisco Kid,'" stiff cardboard window card for "Round Up Show," 1950s, **$250**; John Wayne photo on stiff cardboard store sign advertising Popular Library edition of *The Searchers* book, c. 1955, **$75**; *Rodeo Magazine* from Madison Square Garden with "Daily Events" insert listing appearance of "Rin Tin Tin and his TV Troupe," 1956, **$30**.

1960S TV COWBOYS

"Have Gun Will Travel" board game by Parker Brothers, 1959, **$50**; "Colt .45 Coloring Book," The Saalfield Publishing Co., 1959, **$30**; "The Rifleman Flip Special" cap firing rifle by Hubley, c. 1960, **$150**; Warner Bros.' *Cheyenne,* Little Golden Book published by Simon and Schuster, 1958, **$12**; "Bret and Bart Maverick," pair of die-cut rack cards holding rope tie with a Western motif, metal slide, 1959, each **$35**; "Bat Masterson Coloring Book" by The Saalfield Publishing Co., 1959, **$25**; *F Troop* cast photo cover on pencil tablet by Penworthy, c. 1966, **$25**.

Gunsmoke lunch box with "Marshal" misspelled as "Marshall," Aladdin Industries, Inc., 1959, **$300**; Major Seth Adams (Ward Bond) of *Wagon Train,* Hartland Plastics figure complete with saddle, pistol, rifle, whip, and hat, c. 1960, **$150**; Wyatt Earp (Hugh O'Brian), Hartland Plastics figure complete with saddle, short pistol, long Buntline Special pistol, and hat (correct color is black) c. 1960, **$100**; "Ponderosa Ranch/Nevada," glazed "Regal China" bottle replica of Bonanza homestead that held whiskey by James B. Beam Distilling Co., 1969, **$125**.

PIN-BACK BUTTONS & PREMIUMS

The Lone Ranger Six Gun Ring, General Mills premium, 1947, **$75**; "Topper" lithographed tin tab from set issued by Burry's Hopalong Cassidy Cookies, c. 1950, **$35**; "Tom Mix with Tony/Universal Pictures," c. 1932, **$200**; Lash LaRue," c. 1950, **$35**; "Hopalong Cassidy" lithographed tin tab from set issued by Post's Raisin Bran, c. 1950, **$35**; "Davy Crockett King of the Wild Frontier," c. 1955, **$35**; "Roy Rogers Riders Club," lithographed tin tab, 1952, **$50**; "Gene Autry Deputy Sheriff" brass badge, 1950s, **$250**; "Wild Bill Hickok and Jingles," c. 1955, **$40**; "The Rifleman/Chuck Connors," issued for 16th annual rodeo in Fort Madison, Iowa, 1963, **$60**; "William S. Hart," Autralian issue, c. 1922, $75; "Rin-Tin-Tin Fan Club," 1930s, **$60**; Gabby Hayes Shooting Cannon Ring, Quaker Cereals premium, brass or aluminum barrel, 1951, either **$175**; Tom Mix "Captain" Spur Badge, premium from Ralston Purina, 1941, **$250**; "Bonanza Booster," c. 1960s, **$100**; "Davy Crockett" non-Disney, c. 1955, **$20**; "The Cisco Kid," 1950s, **$75**.

Davy Crockett (Non-Disney)

Such a folk hero was surprisingly overlooked in films prior to the 1950s. A United Artists version of 1950, *Davy Crockett, Indian Scout*, starred George Montgomery. A Universal-International version of 1953, *The Man From The Alamo*, cast Glenn Ford as Crockett. A 1955 Republic film, *The Last Command*, starred Sterling Hayden as Jim Bowie with Arthur Hunnicut in supporting role as Crockett. The 1960 United Artists epic, *The Alamo*, starred John Wayne in the lead role of Crockett. Most unlicensed Davy Crockett merchandise was issued in 1955–1956 to capitalize on the popularity of Disney's TV and film character.

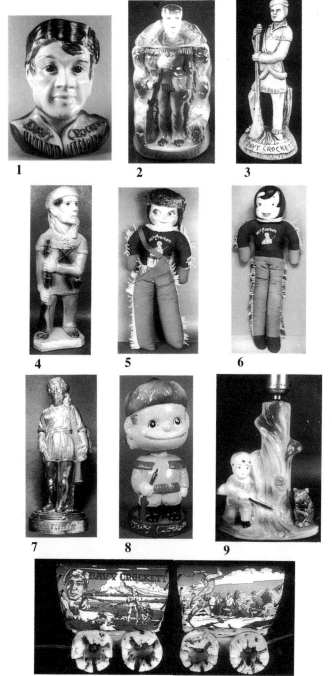

1
DAVY CROCKETT 7x8x10″ tall china cookie jar and lid with C. Miller copyright c. 1955. $400

2
DAVY CROCKETT 7x7x11.5″ tall ceramic cookie jar and lid c. mid-1950s. $300

3
DAVY CROCKETT 10.25″ tall painted solid plaster figure c. mid-1950s. $125

4
DAVY CROCKETT 15.5″ tall painted plaster figure with scattered gold glitter accent c. mid-1950s. $100

5
DAVY CROCKETT 26″ tall stuffed cloth doll with vinyl face and simulated fur coonskin cap c. mid-1950s. $150

6
DAVY CROCKETT 29″ tall stuffed cloth doll with plastic face c. mid-1950s. $100

7
DAVY CROCKETT 11″ tall bronzed metal lamp stand c. mid-1950s. $75

8
DAVY CROCKETT 5.5″ tall composition bobbing head figure c. early 1960s. $200

9
DAVY CROCKETT 4.5x6.5x7.5″ tall china lamp stand c. mid-1950s. $100

10
DAVY CROCKETT 4x5x5.5″ long electrical nightlight in covered wagon image with cardboard cover and dried cactus wheels c. mid-1950s. $150

11

12

13

14

15

16

17

18

19

20

21   **22**   **23**

11
DAVY CROCKETT 11x14″ Saal-field coloring book © 1955. $20

12
DAVY CROCKETT 6x8″ Wonder Book © 1955. $12

13
DAVY CROCKETT 1x3.25x4″ wide case holding chromed identi-fication bracelet plus Crockett club card c. 1955. $60

14
DAVY CROCKETT 2.5x2.5x.75″ deep lithographed metal dime reg-ister bank c. mid-1950s. $125

15
DAVY CROCKETT 3x5″ wide by 6″ tall wooden barrel and diecut figure bank c. mid-1950s. $100

16
DAVY CROCKETT 2.5x4″ wide by 6″ tall copper colored metal slot bank c. mid-1950s. $40

17
DAVY CROCKETT 11x12.5x2″ deep boxed leather holster and belt set by R & S Toy Co. c. 1955. BOXED $100, LOOSE $50

18
DAVY CROCKETT 3.5″ tall flex-ible rubber on plastic base toy with underside crank to make fig-ure move c. mid-1950s. $75

19
DAVY CROCKETT 8″ long tin clicker gun c. mid-1950s. $50

20
ROCKING HORSE 18x22″ tall by 30″ long of wood and plastic by Rich Toys c. 1955. $150

21
"DAVY CROCKETT TIME" 7.5″ dia. painted masonite wall clock c. 1955. $200

22
DAVY CROCKETT 14x23″ litho-graphed metal target with wire ea-sel back c. mid-1950s. $75

23
DAVY CROCKETT 5″ tall clear glass tumbler with color art c. mid-1950s. $15

24
DAVY CROCKETT 2x5x5″ tall
plastic replica figure and horse
with box by Ideal Toy Co. c. mid-
1950s. BOXED $90, LOOSE $50

25
DAVY CROCKETT 7″ dia. replica coonskin hat with plastic
crown and simulated fur bands
and tail c. mid-1950s. $30

26
DAVY CROCKETT 5x6.5″ card
holding 3″ plastic figure and accessories by Product Equipment
Co. c. mid-1950s. $20

27
DAVY CROCKETT 7.5″ long
metal and plastic flashlight with
wrapper card c. mid-1950s.
CARDED $50, LOOSE $25

28
DAVY CROCKETT 3″ long plastic pocket flashlight on keychain
c. mid-1950s. $15

29
DAVY CROCKETT 6.5x8.5x4″
deep steel lunch box and 8.5″ tall
metal bottle set by Holtemp
1955. BOX $140, BOTTLE $60

30
DAVY CROCKETT 8″ tall litho-
graphed metal sand pail by Ohio
Art Co. © 1955. $50

31
"DAVY CROCKETT COOKIES"
2x4.5x8″ long cardboard box in 3-
D image of covered wagon pulled
by oxen c. mid-1950s. $100

32
DAVY CROCKETT 2.5x5x6″
boxed plastic binoculars c. mid-
1950s. BOXED $75, LOOSE $45

33
DAVY CROCKETT 2x7x8″ vinyl
"Bicycle Dispatch Bag" attach-
ment c. mid-1950s. $60

34
DAVY CROCKETT 10″ oval by
9″ tall lithographed tin waste can
c. mid-1950s. $50

35
DAVY CROCKETT 3.25″ tall
white glass mug with single color
art c. mid-1950s. $12

24

25

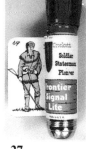

26   **27**

28

29

30

31   **32**

33   **34**   **35**

Death Valley Days

A western drama anthology series, based on fact, that had lengthy runs both as a radio series and subsequent TV series. The radio series was developed through interview recollections of actual citizens and historians of Death Valley in the remote region of California. Noted for historical accuracy throughout, each episode was introduced over the air by The Old Ranger, enacted by at least four individuals through the 1930–1945 continuous run sponsored by 20 Mule Team Borax products. The 1952–1970 TV revival was a similar format to the radio series. Among the Old Ranger portrayers on TV were Ronald Reagan, Robert Taylor, Dale Robertson. Early TV episodes were produced by Gene Autry Flying A Productions.

1

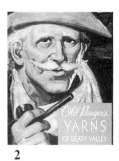

2

3

4

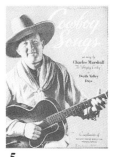

5

6

7

8

9

1
"DEATH VALLEY DAYS" 11x15.5″ four-page "Picture Sheet." Example photo shows upper third of front page and entire back page c. mid-1930s. $10

2
"OLD RANGER'S YARNS" 9x11.5″ booklet by Pacific Coast Borax Co. © 1933. $12

3
"DEATH VALLEY TALES" 9x11.5″ booklet by Pacific Coast Borax Co. © 1934. $15

4
"COWBOY SONGS" 9x12″ folio of songs sung by John White, "The Lonesome Cowboy" of Death Valley Days © 1934. $10

5
"COWBOY SONGS" 9x12″ folio of songs sung by Charles Marshall, "The Singing Cowboy" of Death Valley Days © 1934. $12

6
"DEATH VALLEY DAYS" 8.5x11″ mimeographed typed script for radio episode of April 11, 1935. $30

7
"DEATH VALLEY DAYS" 8.5x11″ publicity and advertising folder by Pacific Coast Borax Co. © 1931. $10

8
DEATH VALLEY 8x10.5″ color jigsaw puzzle premium by Pacific Coast Borax Co. © 1933. $15

9
20 MULE TEAM plastic model assembly kit mail premium with leaflet sent in pair of 2.5x4.5x7.5″ boxes by Pacific Coast Borax Co. c. early 1950s. $30

The Deputy

A half-hour TV series co-starring Henry Fonda, in his first episodic television role, and Allen Case. Fonda portrayed Marshal Simon Fry headquartered in Prescott of the 1880s Arizona Territory. Case portrayed a local storekeeper deputized largely due to his quick draw, gunfight talents. The show began September 12, 1959 and continued through 76 episodes on NBC-TV before ending September 16, 1961.

1
CARD #314 bw 3.25x5.5″ from set of 64 titled ''TV Western Stars'' by Nu Trading Cards c. 1960s. $3

2
THE DEPUTY 10x10.5x2″ boxed set of rigid cardboard holsters, leather belt, metal cap guns by Halco © 1960. BOXED $250, LOOSE $125

3
''THE DEPUTY'' 9.5x19x2″ boxed Milton Bradley board game including ''Deputy Marshal'' badge to be earned by player capturing most outlaws. Example photo shows lid and playing board detail. 1960. $40

4
''THE DEPUTY'' 3x4″ rwb card holding white metal ''Texas Ranger Sheriff'' star badge by Top Gun Co. © 1959. $20

5
THE DEPUTY 3x4″ rwb card holding white metal ''Tombstone/ Helldorado'' star badge by Top Gun Co. © 1959. $20

1

2

3

4

5

F Troop

One of the few humorous western TV series and certainly the most successful, featuring the farcical antics of U.S. Cavalry troop members stationed at Fort Courage following the Civil War. The bumbling and fumbling weekly adventures were usually related to the equally inept Hekawi Tribe of surrounding Indians. Principal stars were Ken Berry as Capt. Wilton Parmenter, Forrest Tucker as Sgt. Morgan O'Rouke, Larry Storch as Cpl. Randolph Agarn, Melody Patterson as Wrangler Jane. The original series began September 14, 1965 and continued through August 31, 1967 on ABC-TV.

1

2

3

1
TV GUIDE 5x7.5″ weekly issue for December 11, 1965. $10

2
TV GUIDE 5x7.5″ weekly issue for August 13, 1966. $10

3
TV GUIDE 5x7.5″ weekly issue for May 27, 1967. $8

4

5

4
F TROOP 9.5x18.5x2″ boxed Ideal Toy Co. board game © 1965. $75

5
F TROOP 6.5x10x1.5″ boxed card game with insert board serving as card tray plus playing surface by Ideal Toy Co. © 1965. $25

6
F TROOP 16.5x19.5x3.5″ boxed ''Magnetic Action'' game featuring 3-D miniature scale replica of Fort Courage with scaled figures and accessories by Multiple Toymakers © 1966. $100

6

7

8

7
F TROOP 7.5x10″ Dell comic book #6 for June 1967. $10

8
AUTOGRAPHED ''MELODY PATTERSON'' 5x7″ bw photo c. mid-1960s. $40

9
AUTOGRAPHED ''FORREST TUCKER'' 5x7″ bw photo c. mid-1960s. $40

10
F TROOP 8.5x11″ Saalfield coloring book © 1966. $25

11
AUTOGRAPHED ''LARRY STORCH' 8x10″ bw photo c. mid-1960s. $40

9

10

11

Fury

A popular Saturday morning live-action children's show centered around the highly intelligent black stallion Fury and youthful Joey Newton, played by Bobby Diamond, chosen by Fury as his sole rider. Adventures were of contemporary nature evolving around the Broken Wheel Ranch operated by Jim Newton, Joey's adoptive father, acted by Peter Graves. The series began October 15, 1955 and continued through 114 original episodes that were partially rerun until the series ended September 3, 1966 on NBC-TV.

1
"FURY/STALLION OF BRO-KEN WHEEL RANCH" 6x8.5" first edition John Winston Co. book © 1959. $15

2
"FURY AND THE LONE PINE MYSTERY" 6x8" Golden Press book © 1959. $15

3
"FURY" 6.75x8" Little Golden Book © 1957. $12

4
"FURY TAKES THE JUMP" 6.75x8" Little Golden Book © 1958. $12

5
"FURY" 5.5x6.5" Whitman Tell-A-Tale book © 1958. $20

6
CARD #217 bw 3.25x5.5" picturing Peter Graves from set of 64 titled "TV Western Stars" by Nu Trading Cards c. 1960s. $3

7
"FURY" 8.5x11" Whitman coloring book © 1958. $25

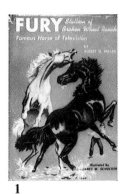

1

2

3

4

5

6

7

George (Gabby) Hayes (1885–1969)

The bewhiskered, cantankerous, irascible and perennial sidekick to Roy Rogers and earlier Bill Elliott, Hopalong Cassidy and others. His western films began in the late 1920s under George Hayes, prior to his popular nickname, and frequently in clean-shaven roles of both good guy and bad guy. He acquired the equally-apt nickname of Windy before settling into the Gabby monicker for most of his career. He was a major supporting star in Roy Rogers movies, radio and TV shows in addition to his own TV series geared to child audiences between December 11, 1950 and July 14, 1956.

1

2

3

4

5

6   7

8   9

1
"GEORGE HAYES" 5x7" tinted bw paper sheet photo with facsimile signature c. 1940s. $30

2
"GABBY HAYES" 3.5x5.5" duotone exhibit card c. 1940s. $8

3
GABBY HAYES 2.25" Dixie Ice Cream cup lid with "Wyoming" film title of 1947. $20

4
GABBY HAYES-BILL ELLIOTT 8x10" Dixie Ice Cream color picture with film title on back from 1943. $35

5
GABBY HAYES 8x10" Dixie Ice Cream color picture with film title "Wyoming" on back from 1947. $35

6
GABBY HAYES 3.5x5.5" Dutch-published color photo card c. 1950. $20

7
GABBY HAYES 3.5x5" bw photo card c. 1940s. $20

8
"TREASURE CHEST OF TALL TALES" 8x11" Wilson-Hill Co. story and activity book © 1952. $25

9
"TALL TALES FOR LITTLE FOLKS" 6.25x8" book with inside front fold-out 17" tall figure that appears in outfit changes as story pages are turned. By Samuel Lowe Co. © 1954. $35

10
"TALL TALE" 8x10.5" Abbott
Co. coloring book c. 1952. $35

11
"GABBY HAYES WESTERN"
7.5x10" Fawcett comic book #14
for January 1950. $25

12
GABBY HAYES 9" tall fabric
hand puppet with hollow soft rubber head finished in brown face
with white beard c. 1950s. $65

13
GABBY HAYES set of five
2.5x7" mail premium comic books
with envelope by Quaker Oats
1951. SET WITH ENVELOPE
$150, EACH $25

14
GABBY HAYES "POPSICLE"
10.25x14" color advertisement
magazine page for contest by TV
series sponsor in 1956. $15

15
GABBY HAYES "WESTERN
GUN" 6x7" boxed mail premium
by Quaker cereals featuring miniature replicas of six-guns plus display board and papers c. early
1950s. BOXED $100, UNBOXED
SET $75

16
GABBY HAYES 9x12" mail pre-
mium envelope holding black felt
"Prospector's Hat" with leaflet
from Quaker cereals c. 1951.
PACKAGED $150, LOOSE $75

17
"GABBY HAYES" 8x10" school
tablet with color cover c. early
1950s. $25

18
GABBY HAYES "COTTON-
TAIL" 10.5x22.5" tall by 30.5"
long wooden rocking horse with
decal portrait c. early 1950s. $150

10

11

12

13

14

15

16

17   **18**

Gene Autry (b. 1907)

The Autry career is said to have begun by his purchase of a $20 guitar for a dollar down and 50¢ monthly payments for the balance. This major purchase and his music talents led him from church choir singer to local entertainer into radio and movie success, culminating in a financial fortune acquired through keen investments.

A Texan by birth and an Oklahoman as a youth, Autry's radio career got underway at Chelsea, Oklahoma, and later Tulsa. His popularity as ''Oklahoma's Yodeling Cowboy'' led him to featured performances on the *National Barn Dance* network radio show, a recording contract, and ultimately to a film contract from Mascot Studio, soon to become Republic Pictures.

His first film appearances in 1934 were supporting roles to star Ken Maynard. His first starring role, both as actor and singer, came in the 1935 Mascot serial *The Phantom Empire*. A prolific song writer as well as cowboy singer, his songs were an integral part of his 1936–1947 years with Republic—interrupted by three years of World War II service—and his final 1948–1953 movie years with Columbia Pictures under his own independent production. In all, Autry starred in more than 90 films and is acknowledged as the first genuine singing cowboy of the screen.

Throughout the years, his films were accented by a sidekick foil, notably Smiley Burnette or Pat Buttram.

Concurrent with his filming, he began his long-running *Gene Autry's Melody Ranch* weekly radio program. Except for his military service years, the program aired steadily for 16 years on CBS following its January 7, 1940 premiere date, all under the continuous single sponsorship of Wrigley's Gum. He and his exquisite ''World Wonder Horse'' Champion were featured at countless fairs, parades and rodeo performances.

Anticipating the oncoming popularity of television, Autry was the first western star to begin filming a series especially for the new medium. Under Gene Autry Flying A Productions, his own show made its debut July 23, 1950 and continued through August 7, 1956. His studio also produced other popular TV western series of *Death Valley Days, The Adventures of Champion, The Range Riders, Buffalo Bill Jr., Annie Oakley*. Other enterprises in recent years have included real estate, oil development, and baseball franchise ownership among a host of successful ventures. In November 1988, the Gene Autry Western Heritage Museum, a $54 million complex, opened in Los Angeles' Griffith Park.

1

2

1
''RADIO RANCH'' set of eight 11x14″ re-issue lobby cards for original 1935 film serial titled ''Phantom Empire.'' SET $175

2
''UNDER FIESTA STARS'' 11x14″ title lobby card for 1941 film. $25

3
''SUNSET IN WYOMING'' 27x41″ one-sheet poster for 1941 film. $200

4
''COWBOY SERENADE'' 27x41″ one-sheet poster for film of 1942. $150

5
''TRAIL TO SAN ANTONE'' 27x41″ one-sheet poster for film of 1947. $100

3   4   5

6
"ROBIN HOOD OF TEXAS"
27x41″ one-sheet poster for film
of 1947. $100

7
"LOADED PISTOLS" 27x41″
one-sheet poster for film of 1949.
$75

8
"RIM OF THE CANYON"
27x41″ one-sheet poster for film
of 1949. $85

9
"COW TOWN" 27x41″ one-sheet
poster for film of 1950. $75

10
"VALLEY OF FIRE" 27x41″
one-sheet poster for film of 1951.
$60

11
"SILVER CANYON" 27x41″
one-sheet poster for film of 1951.
$60

12
"SONS OF NEW MEXICO"
14x36″ insert poster for film of
1950. $50

13
"GOLDTOWN GHOST RID-
ERS" 14x36″ insert poster for
film of 1953. $50

14
"WARNER THEATRE" 10.5x28″
bw paper ad for live appearance c.
1938. $100

15
"MELODY RANCH" 10.5x23.5″
poster for radio show sponsor
Wrigley's Gum also promoting
film "Rancho Grande" c. late
1939-early 1940. $150

16
"DOUBLEMINT WRIGLEY
GUM" 10x12″ cardboard award
easel sign for local merchants c.
early 1940s. $100

6

7

8

9

10

11

12

13

14

15

16

18

17

19

20

17
"SPEAKING FOR AMERICA"
11x14" paper poster from humani-
tarian series for school distribution
c. late 1940s. $35

18
AUTRY 5x8" bw ranch scene
photo with facsimile signature c.
1930s. $25

19
"ROMEO RECORDS" 8x10" bw
photo with record listing on back
c. early 1930s. $40

20
AUTRY 8.5x11" bw photo of
probable issue by radio station c.
1930s. $20

21
AUTRY 8.5x11" bw photo of
probable issue by radio station c.
1930s. $20

22
"WHEATIES" 6.25x8.25" back
panel from cereal box c. late
1936-early 1937. $35

23
"GENE AUTRY CLUB" 5x6.75"
mailing card picturing club button
offered for purchase of clothing
merchandise listed on back c.
early 1950s. $50

24
AUTRY 4.75x5.5" "Autograph
Album" closed leaflet that opens
to photos and club membership
panel c. 1940s. $125

25
AUTRY 2.25" Dixie Ice Cream
cup lid with film title from 1937.
$20

26
AUTRY 2.25" Dixie Ice Cream
cup lid with film title from 1938.
$15

27
AUTRY 2.75" Dixie Ice Cream
cup lid with film title from 1948.
$10

21   **22**   **23**

24

25   **26**   **27**

28
AUTRY 8x10″ Dixie Ice Cream color picture with movie title on back from 1937. $30

29
AUTRY 8x10″ Dixie Ice Cream color picture with movie titles on back from 1937-1938. $25

30
AUTRY 4x5.5″ laminated color photo masonite plaque c. 1940s. $25

31
AUTRY 4.5x5.5″ laminated bw photo masonite plaque c. 1940s. $25

32
''PRAIRIE MOON'' 5x7″ bw Republic Picture photo with 1938 film title. $12

33
AUTRY 8x10″ bw press release photo from live appearance for children with back caption including ''Blazing Sun'' movie title and October 27, 1950 photo release date. $20

34
''GENE AUTRY AND CHAMP JR.'' 6x11″ tissue sheet with reverse image transfer picture c. 1940s. $20

35
AUTRY 8x10″ paper portrait stamped for distribution by local clothing store c. 1940s. $25

36
AUTRY 3.5x5.5″ European bw postcard c. 1950s. $12

37
AUTRY 3.5x5.5″ sepia photo postcard from English ''Picture-goer'' series c. 1950s. $12

38
AUTRY 3.5x5.5″ color postcard published in Holland c. 1950s. $12

39
AUTRY 3.5x5.5″ color postcard published in Holland c. 1950s. $12

28

29

30

31

32

33

34

35

36

37

38

39

40

41

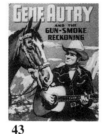

43

46

47

45

50

51

52

53

40
"HOME OF GENE AUTRY"
3.5x5″ color postcard c. 1940s. $8

41
AUTRY & OTHERS 8.5x12″ display card for Exhibit Card vending machine c. 1940s. $30

42
"EMPRESS HALL" 7.5x10″ publicity sheet for live performance in London, England July 27, 1953. $30

43
AUTRY 3.5x4.5″ Whitman Better Little Book #1434 © 1943. $35

44
AUTRY 3.5x4.5″ Whitman Better Little Book #1409 © 1946. $25

45
AUTRY 3.5x5.5″ Whitman Big Little Book © 1950. $20

46
"MOUNTAIN BROADCAST" 8.5x11″ radio magazine with cover article about Autry in military service and September 1945 publication date. $15

47
"MELODY RANCH" 11x14″ Whitman cut-out doll book © 1951. $50

48
"GUN SMOKE YARNS" 4.25x6.5″ Dell paperback with stories selected by Autry © 1948. $12

49
AUTRY 10x15″ Merrill Co. coloring book © 1940. $40

50
AUTRY 10x15″ Merrill Co. coloring book © 1941. $35

51
AUTRY 11x15″ Whitman coloring book © 1949. $30

52
AUTRY 11x15″ Whitman coloring book © 1950. $30

53
AUTRY 8x11″ Whitman coloring book © 1952. $40

54
"THIEF RIVER OUTLAWS"
6x8" Whitman book © 1944. $15

55
"REDWOOD PIRATES" 6x8"
Whitman book © 1946. $15

56
"GOLDEN LADDER GANG"
6x8" Whitman book © 1950. $15

57
"BIG VALLEY GRAB" 6x8"
Whitman book © 1952. $20

58
"GOLDEN STALLION" 6x8"
Whitman book © 1954. $20

59
"GHOST RIDERS" 6x8" Whit-
man book © 1955. $20

60
"ARAPAHO WAR DRUMS"
6x8" Whitman book © 1957. $20

61
AUTRY 5.25x7.5" Sandpiper
Book © 1951. $25

62
AUTRY 6.5x8" Little Golden
Book © 1955. $15

63
AUTRY 5.5x6.5" Whitman Tell-
A-Tale book © 1952. $20

64
AUTRY 5.5x6.5" Whitman Tell-
A-Tale book © 1953. $20

65
TV GUIDE 5.5x8.5" weekly issue
for May 17, 1952. $45

66
AUTRY 8.5x11" program from
traveling tour performances of
1949. $40

67
AUTRY 8.5x11" program from
traveling tour performances of
1951. $35

68
AUTRY 8.5x11" program from
traveling tour performances of
early 1950s. $30

54

55

56

57

58

59

60

61

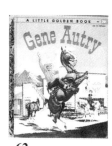

62

63

64

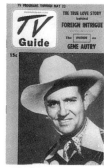

65

66

67

68

69

70

71

72

73

74

75

76

77

78

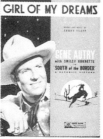

79

80

69
''PUBLICITY PORTFOLIO''
9.5x12.5″ folder kit of pre-publicity and advertising materials for live performances at local fairs in 1960 season. $100

70
''GENE AUTRY COMICS''
7.5x10″ Fawcett Vol. 1 #4 issue for January 8, 1943. $165

71
''GENE AUTRY COMICS''
7.5x10″ Dell Vol. 1 #96 issue for Februrary 1955. $10

72
''GENE AUTRY AND CHAMPION'' 7.5x10″ Dell comic book Vol. 1 #116 for October-December 1957. $5

73
''GENE AUTRY ADVENTURE COMICS'' 6.5x8″ ''Play-Fun'' Pillsbury premium booklet © 1947. $75

74
AUTRY 2.5x7″ premium comic booklet from set of five by Quaker Cereals 1950. EACH $30

75
AUTRY 9x12″ sheet music © 1935. $15

76
AUTRY 9x12″ sheet music © 1935. $15

77
AUTRY 9x12″ sheet music © 1935. $15

78
AUTRY 9x12″ sheet music for theme song of Melody Ranch radio program © 1937. $25

79
AUTRY 9x12″ sheet music © 1939. $12

80
AUTRY 9x12″ sheet music © 1939. $12

81
AUTRY 9x12″ sheet music
© 1945. $12

82
AUTRY 9x12″ sheet music
© 1949. $20

83
"BOOK NO. 2" 9x12″ song folio
© 1934. $25

84
"DE LUXE EDITION" 9x12″
song folio © 1938. $25

85
"SONGS GENE AUTRY
SINGS" 9x12″ folio © 1942. $20

86
"COWBOY SONGS" 9x13″ folio
with Autry cover c. 1940s. $20

87
"COWBOY SONGS" 10.5x12″
album of four 78 rpm OKeh records c. late 1930s. $60

88
"WESTERN CLASSICS"
10.5x12″ album of 78 rpm Columbia records © 1947. $40

89
"CHAMPION" 10x10″ album of
two 78 rpm Columbia records c.
early 1950s. $20

90
AUTRY CHRISTMAS 10x10″
dust cover with 78 rpm Columbia
record © 1950. $12

91
"RUDOLPH, THE RED-NOSED
REINDEER" 10x10″ album holding 78 rpm Columbia record
© 1949. $20

92
AUTRY DRUM SET with 19.5″
dia. central drum and all drums
formed in combination of taut
cardboard, fabric and metal by
Colmor Co. c. 1940s. $250

93
AUTRY 31″ tall plastic guitar
with carrying case and 16-page
song booklet by Emenee Industries
c. 1955. BOXED $150, LOOSE
$75

81

82

83

84

85

86

87

88

89

90

91
92

93

94

95

96

97

98

99

100

101

102

94
"GENE AUTRY/MELODY RANCH" 36″ tall pressed wood guitar c. early 1940s. $175

95
"GENE AUTRY" 12″ tall painted solid composition figure c. 1940s. $400

96
"STRINGLESS MARIONETTE" 14.5″ tall fabric and rubber full figure hand puppet with box by National Mask & Puppet Corp. c. 1951. BOXED $125, LOOSE $75

97
"BANDIT TRAIL" 10x19x2″ boxed board game c. late 1930s. $150

98
"GENE AUTRY/CHAMPION" 8x11.5x1.5″ boxed "Ranch Outfit" of cardboard holster, composition gun, leather belt, fabric neckerchief, cord lasso by M. A. Henry Co. © 1941. $150, IF WITH COMPOSITION GUN $200

99
AUTRY 6″ long snub-nosed cast iron cap pistol with white plastic grips in box c. late 1930s. BOXED $250, LOOSE $150

100
AUTRY 6″ long snub-nosed cast iron cap pistol with orange plastic grips by Kenton Toys c. late 1930s. $150

101
AUTRY 9″ long silvered metal cap pistol with red plastic grips in 4x8.5x1.5″ box by Kenton Toys c. 1940s. BOXED $300, UNBOXED $175

102
AUTRY 8.5″ long silvered cast iron cap gun with white marbled plastic grips by Kenton Toys c. 1940s. $150

103
AUTRY 8″ long silvered metal cap pistol with white plastic grips in 1.5x3.5x8″ box by Leslie-Henry Co. c. 1950s. BOXED $200, UNBOXED $125

104
"CHAMPION" 9″ long gold finished metal cap pistol with black plastic grips by Leslie-Henry Co. c. 1950s. BOXED (SAME AS #103) $225, UNBOXED $125

105
AUTRY 9″ long gold finished metal cap pistol with white plastic grips in 5x9x1.5″ box by Leslie-Henry Co. c. early 1950s. BOXED $225, UNBOXED $125

106
AUTRY 7″ long "Rootin' Tootin' Pistol Horn" metal attachment with rubber squeeze handle for bicycle handlebar c. 1950s. BOXED $90, LOOSE $50

107
AUTRY 8″ long cardboard rubber band guns plus cardboard targets from Autry "Riders Of The West" membership kit c. 1953. $75

108
"FLYING A RANCH" 9.5″ long brown leather holster set c. 1940s. $75

109
AUTRY 9.5″ brown leather holster from set c. 1946. $50

110
"FLYING A RANCH" 11″ long black leather double holster set with metal gun covers c. 1950s. $175

111
"JEANS AND SHIRTS" 8.25x11″ back cover ad from rodeo program c. 1947. $35

112
AUTRY "COWBOY BELTS" 8x10x2″ deep box originally holding 12 brown tooled leather belts c. 1940s. BOX $75, BELT $50

103

104

105

106

107

108

109

110

111

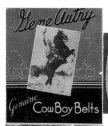

112

114

115

113

117

116

118

119

120

121

122

123

113
AUTRY 4x4.5″ simulated leather embossed zippered wallet c. 1940s. $40

114
AUTRY 3.5x4.5″ plastic wallet c. 1950s. $40

115
AUTRY 3.25x5.25″ carded silvered metal "Horseshoe Nail Ring" with engraved Autry signature c. 1940s. CARDED $125, LOOSE $75

116
"GENE AUTRY WATCH" engraved on reverse "Always Your Pal-Gene Autry" c. 1948. $175

117
"SIX SHOOTER" 2.5x6″ boxed wristwatch with animated gun hand on dial face that moves each second c. 1951. BOXED $400, LOOSE $200

118
AUTRY 10x11x4″ boxed set of child's leather cowboy boots with Autry name on each elastic pull strap c. 1950. BOXED $350, LOOSE $150

119
AUTRY 7.5″ tall set of child's rubber galoshes with color art on outer side of each c. 1950. $150

120
AUTRY & CHAMP 10x26″ felt pennant c. 1940s. $50

121
AUTRY & CHAMP 11x28″ felt pennant c. 1940s. $50

122
AUTRY 6.5x10″ spiral-bound cardboard "Stencil Book" album of western designs c. 1950s. $50

123
AUTRY 8x12.5″ cardboard panel holding erasable film sheet plus wood stylus by Lowe Co. c. 1950s. $40

124
AUTRY 9.25x11.5″ frame tray in-lay jigsaw puzzle in original clear wrap by Whitman c. 1950s. $30

125
AUTRY 5.5x9″ school tablet with color cover c. 1950s. $20

126
AUTRY 5.5x9″ school tablet with color cover c. 1950s. $20

127
AUTRY 4x6.25x2″ boxed hair-brushes with early plastic handles c. 1940s. BOXED $175, EACH BRUSH $50

128
"MELODY RANCH" 6.5x9x3.5″ deep steel lunch box and 8.5″ steel bottle set by Universal Co. 1954. BOX $250, BOTTLE $100

129
AUTRY 5.25″ long brass and plastic mechanical pencil with clear segment in barrel center of Autry on Champion that lights when pencil cap is pulled down c. 1940s. $50

130
AUTRY 2.75″ square waxed paper bread loaf end labels from 1950s series. EACH $15

131
AUTRY 3.25″ tall enameled metal pocket flashlight c. 1950s. $40

132
"SOUVENIR OF RODEO" 1.75″ celluloid button suspending vinyl holster holding metal replica six-shooter c. 1940s. $35

133
AUTRY & CHAMP 1.75″ cellu-loid button c. 1940s. $25

134
AUTRY 3″ lithographed tin button from cowboy "Film Caravan" 1987 convention. $10

135
AUTRY 2.5″ celluloid button from cowboy "Film Caravan" 1987 convention. $10

124

125

126

127

128

129

130

131

132

133

134

135

The Gray Ghost

A television drama based on the actual exploits during the Civil War of Confederate Major John Singleton Mosby of the First Virginia Cavalry, known for his effective guerilla organization and leadership leading to his "Gray Ghost" reputation. The TV Major Mosby was portrayed by Tod Andrews throughout the 39 episodes syndicated in 1957 by CBS Film Sales.

1

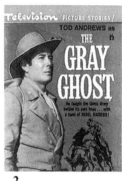

2

1
"VIDEO GUIDE" 5.5x8.25" weekly issue for September 28, 1958 including articles on four other current TV western series. $20

2
"THE GRAY GHOST" 5.5x7.25" comic book published by CBS Television Film Sales for distribution in Australia © 1958. $50

3
"THE GRAY GHOST" 9x17.5x1.5" boxed Transogram board game © 1958. $60

4
"THE GRAY GHOST" 9x10.5" cardboard panel with spiral-bound album of 12 pre-printed erasable illustrations to be colored plus erasable film sheet and crayons by Transogram © 1958. $40

5
"THE GRAY GHOST" 10x12x2" boxed gray leather bullet cartridge belt and holster holding 10" silvered metal cap gun with dark amber plastic grips c. 1958. BOXED $350, LOOSE $150

3

4

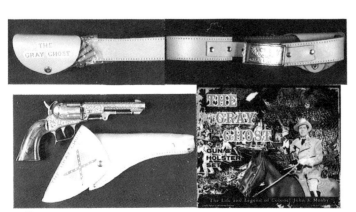

5

Gunsmoke

Television's longest-running western series, also credited as TV's longest-running prime time series, with continuing characters after completing its unbroken 1955–1975 CBS 20-year run. Based on a radio series of the same title that began in 1952 starring William Conrad, the TV version eventually made a household name of James Arness as Marshal Matt Dillon of Dodge City, Kansas. The soft-spoken lumbering style of Arness (chosen for the role originally declined by John Wayne) was accented weekly by his steadfast Dodge City cronies including sidekick Chester Goode, female interest Miss Kitty and crusty Doc Adams.

1
TV GUIDE 5x7.5″ weekly issue for March 15, 1958. $30

2
TV GUIDE 5x7.5″ weekly issue for January 2, 1960. $25

3
TV GUIDE 5x7.5″ weekly issue for December 10, 1960. $25

4
TV GUIDE 5x7.5″ weekly issue for June 12, 1965. $20

5
TV GUIDE 5x7.5″ weekly issue for December 10, 1966. $15

6
"TV HEADLINER" 8x10.5″ November 1958 issue of fan magazine. $40

7
AUTOGRAPHED "JIM ARNESS" 8x10″ bw photo. $30

8
JAMES ARNESS 3.5x5.5″ bw exhibit card c. 1960s. $5

9
CARD #317 bw 3.25x5″ from set of 64 titled "TV Western Stars" by Nu Trading Cards c. 1960s. $3

10
ARNESS-AMANDA BLAKE 21x22″ cardboard sign for L&M Cigarettes by Liggett & Myers Tobacco Co. c. late 1950s. $100

11
ARNESS-AMANDA BLAKE 21x21″ cardboard sign similar to item #10. $100

12
"GUNSMOKE" 2.5x3.5″ card from series of 15 within 71-card "T.V. Westerns" set by Topps Gum Co. 1958. EACH $5

1

2

3

4

5

6

7

8

9

10

11

12

13

14

15

16

17

18

19

20

21

22

23

24

25

13
GUNSMOKE 8.5x11″ Whitman coloring book © 1959. $30

14
GUNSMOKE 6x8″ Whitman book © 1958. $20

15
GUNSMOKE 6.5x8″ Little Golden Book © 1958. $15

16
GUNSMOKE 7.5x10.5″ annual book published in England 1958. $35

17
GUNSMOKE 8.5x11″ annual book published in England 1964. $35

18
GUNSMOKE 8.5x11″ annual book published in England 1965. $25

19
GUNSMOKE 8.5x11″ annual book published in England 1966. $25

20
GUNSMOKE 8x11″ annual book published in England 1974. $25

21
"MATT DILLON" 7x11.5″ carded 4″ tall figure and horse by Hartland Plastics Co. © 1960. CARDED $90, LOOSE $50

22
"MATT DILLON" 8.5x9.5x3.5″ boxed full sized replica figure with horse and accessories by Hartland Plastics Co. c. 1960. BOXED $250, LOOSE $125

23
GUNSMOKE 12x14x2″ boxed tooled leather belt and holster holding 9.5″ long metal cap gun by Halco © 1956. BOXED $275, LOOSE $150

24
GUNSMOKE 6x12x2″ boxed 11″ cap gun plus plastic clip with six brass bullets by Halco c. 1956. BOXED $200, LOOSE $100

25
GUNSMOKE 12x20x5″ playset by Prestige Toy © 1958. $175

26
GUNSMOKE 11x14″ boxed fabric outfit with Marshal badge © 1958. BOXED $125, LOOSE $75

27
GUNSMOKE 3x7″ fabric and vinyl gloves with "U.S. Marshal" brass badge on each gauntlet c. late 1950s. $30

28
GUNSMOKE 4.5x4.5″ packaged set of three View-Master reels © 1972. $25

29
"JAMES ARNESS AS MATT DILLON" 8x10″ school tablet with color cover c. late 1950s. $20

30
"AMANDA BLAKE" 8x10″ school tablet with color cover c. late 1950s. $15

31
GUNSMOKE 11.25x14.5″ frame tray inlay jigsaw puzzle by Whitman © 1958. $25

32
GUNSMOKE 7x8x4″ deep steel lunch box by Aladdin Industries © 1959. BOX $125, BOTTLE $60

33
GUNSMOKE 7x9x2″ boxed Whitman 63-piece jigsaw puzzle c. 1960s. $20

34
GUNSMOKE 7x8x4″ deep steel lunch box with embossed front by Aladdin Industries © 1962. BOX $125, BOTTLE $60

35
GUNSMOKE 11.5x14.5″ frame tray inlay jigsaw puzzle by Whitman c. 1959. $20

36
GUNSMOKE 7x8x4″ deep steel lunch box by Aladdin Industries © 1972. BOX $85, BOTTLE $35

37
GUNSMOKE 8x11x2″ boxed 100-piece Whitman jigsaw puzzle c. 1960s. $20

26

27

28

29

30

Note: *31* appears here

32

33

34

35

36

37

Have Gun, Will Travel

A very enduring western TV series, known equally well as the ''Paladin'' series due to the effectiveness in that starring role of Richard Boone. Paladin's soldier-of-fortune services were begun weekly for a recipient of his ''Have Gun-Will Travel. Wire Paladin, San Francisco'' business card with chess knight symbol. The intriguing nature of Paladin ranged from his intellectual tastes as a white-suited resident of San Francisco's Hotel Carlton to his grim black-suited alter ego as a paid gunfighter. The show aired on CBS from September 14, 1957 to September 21, 1963.

1
TV GUIDE 5x7.5″ weekly issue for May 10, 1958. $20

2
TV GUIDE 5x7.5″ weekly issue for February 28, 1959. $15

3
TV GUIDE 5x7.5″ weekly issue for February 6, 1960. $15

4
AUTOGRAPHED ''RICHARD BOONE'' 5x7″ bw photo c. late 1950s. $30

5
CARD #7 bw 3.25x5″ from set of 64 titled ''TV Western Stars'' by Nu Trading Cards c. 1960s. $3

6
''HAVE GUN, WILL TRAVEL'' 6x8″ Whitman book © 1958. $20

7
''HAVE GUN WILL TRAVEL'' 8.5x11″ Lowe Co. coloring book © 1960. $30

8
DELL comic book #931 from 1958. $35

9
DELL comic book #1044 for October-December 1959. $25

10
PALADIN 7″ tall figure with horse and accessories by Hartland Plastics Co. c. 1960. BOXED $300, LOOSE $150

11
PALADIN 6.5x11″ carded figure 4″ tall with hat and horse by Hartland Plastics Co. © 1960. CARDED $100, LOOSE $50

12
PALADIN 8″ tall replica figure by Hartland Plastics Co. c. 1960. BOXED $300, LOOSE $200

13
"PALADIN CHECKERS"
12.5x16″ carded set by Ideal Toy
Co. © 1960. $75

14
"HAVE GUN, WILL TRAVEL"
10x19x1.5″ boxed Parker Brothers
board game © 1959. $50

15
"HAVE GUN WILL TRAVEL"
12x14″ boxed set of black leather
belt and double holsters plus plastic canteen and packet of business
cards by Halco c. 1960. BOXED
$200, LOOSE $75

16
"HAVE GUN WILL TRAVEL"
5x8″ pack holding miniature Derringer pistol with holster, business
cards and card case by Halco
© 1960. $100

17
PALADIN 9″ long set of black
leather holsters trimmed in white
with metal chess knight disk on
each holster cover c. 1960. $50

18
PALADIN 16x18″ carded "Western Outfit" of thin plastic mask,
vinyl vest and simulated bullet
clip, tie ring, packet of business
cards. By Ben Cooper Co.
© 1959. $150

19
"HAVE GUN WILL TRAVEL"
12x13x3.5″ tall black felt hat with
silver/black fabric replica business
card label on crown front. By Arlington Hat Co. c. 1958. $75

20
"HAVE GUN WILL TRAVEL"
12x13x3.5″ tall tan straw hat with
same label as #19. By Arlington
Hat Co. c. 1958. $60

21
"HAVE GUN WILL TRAVEL"
2x5.5″ card holding plastic ring
topped by chess knight symbol
© 1958 in cellophane sleeve.
PACKAGED $50, LOOSE $25

22
"HAVE GUN WILL TRAVEL"
12x20x5″ boxed playset by Prestige Toy © 1958. $175

13

14

15

16

17

18

19   **20**

21   **22**

23

25   **26**

27

23
''PALADIN KIT'' 2.5x4.25″ enveloped set of black felt mustache and four Paladin business cards by Arlington Hat Co. c. 1958. $35

24
PALADIN 2.5x4″ vinyl folder holding business cards and fan club card c. 1958. $35

25
''HAVE GUN WILL TRAVEL'' 7″ long set of child's fabric and vinyl gloves with metal chess knight symbol on each gauntlet c. late 1950s. $25

26
''HAVE GUN WILL TRAVEL'' 8.5x13″ card holding erasable film sheet and wood stylus for marking © 1960. $50

27
''RICHARD BOONE'' 8x9.5″ color photo c. 1958. $15

28
''RICHARD BOONE'' 8x12″ school tablet with color cover c. 1958. $35

29
PALADIN 3.5″ celluloid button in packet from ''Top Western T.V. Stars'' series © 1958. $60

30
PALADIN 7x8x4″ deep steel lunch box and 6.5″ tall steel bottle set by Aladdin Industries © 1960. BOX $200, BOTTLE $100

31
''HAVE GUN, WILL TRAVEL'' 2.5x3.5″ card from series of seven in 71-card ''T.V. Westerns'' set by Topps Gum 1958. EACH $3

28

29

30   **31**

Hoot Gibson (1892–1962)

Edmund Richard Gibson became "Hoot" as a pre-teen youngster, according to legend, from his frequent pastime of hunting owls. A runaway as soon as he became a teenager, Gibson drifted from circus work to cowpunching to stuntman in cowboy tour shows before his first minor film role in 1911. His western film career got underway in 1916 and continued into 1944. He returned for a cameo role in the sprawling 1959 western film *The Horse Soldiers* and totaled 124 western film credits. Gibson was an atypical cowboy hero. Unlike others, he injected humor into his roles. His style was of a commoner, not adept as a gunfighter, fistfighter or lady's man. Nevertheless his popularity as a cowboy star in the late 1920s ran second only to Tom Mix.

1
"HOOT GIBSON" 2x3.25″ card from 80-card "Stars Of The Movie World" set by American Caramel Co. c. 1920s. $8

2
"ROPE SPINNING" 5x6″ instruction booklet for use with the "Hoot Gibson Rodeo Rope" © 1929. $35

3
AUTOGRAPHED "HOOT GIBSON" 8x10″ bw photo c. 1940s. $125

4
"THE CALGARY STAMPEDE" 5.5x8″ book based on movie of same title © 1925. $25

5
"HOOT GIBSON" 7.5x10″ Fox Features comic book #5 from June 1950. $50

6
"HOOT GIBSON'S WESTERN ROUNDUP" 7.5x10″ Fox Features "Giant" comic book with 132 pages © 1950. $80

7
"HOOT GIBSON" 2.25″ Dixie Ice Cream cup lid with title "Feud Of The West." 1936. $15

8
"HOOT GIBSON" 3.5x5.5″ exhibit card c. 1940s. $5

9
"HOOT GIBSON" leather holster and cartridge belt c. 1930s. $50

10
CHILD'S OUTFIT of shirt, chaps, stiff fabric holster and belt. Shirt has "Universal Jewel Ranch" patch. 1930s. $175

HOOT GIBSON
Starring in Universal Pictures

1

2

3

4

5

6

7

8

9

10

Hopalong Cassidy (William Boyd 1898–1972)

Hopalong Cassidy was a foul-mouthed, irascible heavy-drinking old reprobate who limped "hop-along" style from a gunfight wound. At least that was the concept of his original creator, novelist Clarence Mulford, in the early 1900s. The Mulford version underwent an identity change beginning with the first Hopalong Cassidy movie in 1935. The "new" Cassidy was William Boyd, a prematurely white-haired soft-spoken, actually gallant champion of western justice. Boyd, a popular leading man in silent non-western films throughout the 1920s, drew his first notable cowboy role in the 1931 classic *The Painted Desert* co-starring a newcomer named Clark Gable as the villain; but Boyd's prominence as a cowboy star began with the 1935 Hopalong series produced by Harry Sherman. The Boyd and Sherman pact resulted in more than 65 Hopalong films over a 10-year period. Boyd became his own producer in the mid-1940s and had the foresight to acquire television rights to the Cassidy character from creator Mulford plus Paramount and United Artists studios. Hopalong films, adapted for TV length, began in 1948. By 1950–1951, Boyd as Cassidy had enthralled a new generation of fans numbering in the millions. By 1951, the Hoppy image had appeared on almost every conceivable type of merchandise for youngsters. At the height of popularity in the early 1950s, a known 63 TV stations carried the series in addition to more than 150 radio stations broadcasting the audio versions; more than 150 newspapers ran the Hopalong comic strip; more than 200 manufacturers are estimated as licensed makers of Hopalong items. In the late 1950s Boyd sold the rights to Hopalong after amassing a personal fortune, much of it passed along in gratitude to orphanages and children's hospitals.

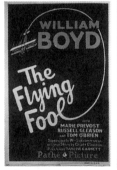

1

2

3

1
"THE FLYING FOOL" 27x41″ non-western movie poster 1929. $250

2
"THE EAGLE'S BROOD" 27x41″ movie poster 1935. $350

3
"BAR 20 JUSTICE" 27x41″ re-issue movie poster for original 1938 film. $90

4

5

6

4
"THE MARAUDERS" 27x41″ movie poster 1947. $150

5
"SINISTER JOURNEY" 27x41″ movie poster 1947. $100

6
"BORROWED TROUBLE" 27x41″ movie poster 1948. $150

7
"DANGEROUS VENTURE" 22x28″ movie poster 1947. $75

8
"THE DEAD DON'T DREAM" 22x28″ movie poster 1947. $75

7   8

9
"PUBLICITY AND EXPLOITA-
TION" 10x14" pressbook for
Harry Sherman distribution of
Hoppy films c. early 1940s. $50

10
"COLE BROS. CIRCUS" 17x26"
cardboard sign c. 1947. $300

11
HOPPY 6x11.5" monthly 12-sheet
calendar for 1952. $200

12
AUTOGRAPHED 3.5x5.5" bw
postcard c. 1950. $150

13
"WILLIAM BOYD" 2.75" Dixie
Ice Cream lid. 1930s. $20

14
"WILLIAM BOYD" 2.25" Dixie
Ice Cream lid. 1930s. $20

15
"WILLIAM BOYD" 2.75" Dixie
Ice Cream with "Border Vigi-
lantes" title. 1941. $15

16
"WILLIAM BOYD" 5x7" tinted
bw thin paper photo from dime
store picture frame c. 1940. $25

17
PARAMOUNT PICTURES 5x7"
bw photo card c. early 1940s. $20

18
"WM. BOYD" 3.5x5.5" exhibit
card c. early 1940s. $10

19
"BILL BOYD" 3.5x5.5" exhibit
card c. 1940s. $10

20
"BILL BOYD/HOP-A-LONG
CASSIDY" 8x10" tinted photo in
dime store frame. 1940s. $50

21
PREMIUM PHOTO 7x8.5" bw for
Barclay Knitwear Co. © 1949.
$30

22
"HOPALONG CASSIDY SE-
RIES" 3.5x5.5" English color
postcard c. 1950s. $20

23
CHRYSLER-PLYMOUTH 3x5"
bw ad postcard 1942. $20

9   10   11

12   13   14

15   16   17

18   19   20

21   22   23

24

25

26

27

28

29

30

31

32

33

34

35

36

24
"HOME OF HOPALONG CAS-SIDY" 3.5x5.5" color postcard c. 1950s. $35

25
HOPPY 6x10" wood framed plaque personalized by department store photo of youngster at his side c. early 1950s. $100

26
HOPPY 7" long diecut stiff paper pistol published by Buzza Cardozo, Hollywood c. 1951. $35

27
HOPPY 4x5" birthday card with diecut front cover window opening c. 1951. $30

28
HOPPY 5.25x6" birthday card with inner front disk wheel to change views in diecut cover opening c. 1951. $25

29
HOPPY 5.25x6" birthday card of same concept as #28 c. 1951. $25

30
HOPPY 5.25x6" birthday card of same concept as #28 c. 1951. $25

31
"LIFE" 10x13" issue for June 12, 1950. $20

32
"TIME" 8.25x11" issue for November 27, 1950. $25

33
"QUICK" 4.25x6" issue for May 1, 1950. $35

34
"TV DIGEST" 5.25x8.25" issue for November 29, 1952. $75

35
"TELE-VIEWS" 5.5x8.5" issue for February 1, 1951. $75

36
"THE BAR-20 THREE" 5.5x7.5" Mulford novel including Hopalong character © 1921. $30

37
"BUCK PETERS, RANCH-
MAN" 5.5x7.5" Mulford novel
including Hoppy character
© 1912 c. 1920s. $30

38
"HOPALONG CASSIDY RE-
TURNS" 4x6" paperback Mulford
novel © 1946. $20

39
"HOPALONG CASSIDY'S
WESTERN" 7x10" Vol. 1 #1
pulp magazine for Fall 1950. $125

40
HOPPY 5.5x8" reprint edition
Mulford novel c. 1950. $25

41
HOPPY 5.5x8" reprint edition
Mulford novel c. 1950. $25

42
HOPPY 5.5x8" reprint edition
Mulford novel c. 1950. $25

43
HOPPY 11x13.5" Doubleday coloring book © 1950. $50

44
HOPPY 8.5x11" Doubleday color-
ing book sponsored by "Acrobat
Shoes" © 1950. $50

45
HOPPY 11x13" Abbott coloring
book © 1951. $50

46
HOPPY 11x13" Lowe coloring
book © 1950. $50

47
HOPPY 8x11" Doubleday "Television Book" with disk wheel that
changes images © 1950. $45

48
HOPPY 6.75x8" Little Golden
Book © 1952. $20

49
HOPPY 6.5x8" Doubleday book
© 1950. $25

50
HOPPY 7.5x8" Whitman book
© 1951. $25

51
HOPPY 8x11" "Stories No. 1"
English book from series of four.
Early 1950s. EACH $40

37

38

39

40

41

42

43

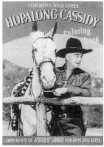

44

45

46

47

48

49

50

51

52

53

54

55

56

57

58

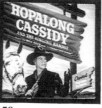

59

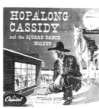

60

61

62

63

64   **65**

52
''HOPALONG CASSIDY''
7.5x10″ Fawcett comic book #23
for September 1948. $60

53
''HOPALONG CASSIDY''
15x18″ original art by Dan Spiegle
for 1951 comic book. $300

54
HOPPY 9x12″ Paramount Music
song folio © 1940. $40

55
''SONG & SADDLE'' 8x10″
western music folio © 1947. $40

56
''HOPALONG CASSIDY
MARCH'' 9x12″ sheet music
© 1951. $75

57
HOPPY 10x10″ Capitol Records
album with 78 rpm adventure
record c. early 1950s. $50

58
''MY HORSE TOPPER''
10x10.5″ Little Folks Favorites album with 78 rpm record c. late
1940s. $30

59
HOPPY 12x12″ Capitol Records
album with related illustrated story
script © 1950. $50

60
HOPPY 10.5x12″ Capitol Records
album with related illustrated story
script © 1950. $60

61
''BIG RANCH FIRE'' 7x7″ Capitol Records paper album with 45
rpm record c. early 1950s. $50

62
''HAPPY BIRTHDAY'' from
same series as #61. $50

63
''MAIL TRAIN ROBBERY''
from same series as #61. $50

64
''HAUNTED GOLD MINE''
from same series as #61. $50

65
HOPPY 9.5″ long Capitol Records
premium cardboard pop pistol c.
early 1950s. $75

66
HOPPY & TOPPER 5x5x2.25″ boxed hard plastic replica figures by Ideal Toy Co. c. 1950. BOXED $200, LOOSE $125

67
HOPPY & TOPPER 2″ tall painted metal replica figures made in England c. 1950. $250

68
"WESTERN SERIES" of seven 2.25″ tall painted metal figures by Timpo of England in original box c. early 1950s. $500

69
HOPPY 11″ tall hand puppet with fabric body and painted soft rubber head © 1951. $100

70
HOPPY 22″ tall stuffed cloth doll with child's vinyl face c. early 1950s. $250

71
HOPPY 4″ tall plastic bank with removable hat c. 1951. $35

72
"HOP A' LONG CASSIDY" 2.5x9.5x11″ long lithographed tin wind-up rocker toy by Marx Toys c. 1950. $350

73
"SHOOTING GALLERY" 14x16.5x5″ boxed lithographed tin gun and target toy with wind-up feature to produce target movement. By Automatic Toy Co. c. early 1950s. BOXED $350, LOOSE $150

74
"ORIGINAL HOPALONG" 46.5″ tall steel rod and spring pogo stick c. early 1950s. $250

75
"TOPPER" 18x19″ tall inflatable vinyl toy c. early 1950s. $125

76
"TOPPER" 12x39x27″ tall hard plastic and wood rocking horse by Rich Toys c. early 1950s. $250

66

67

68

69

70

71

72

73

74

75

76

77

78

79

80

81

82

83

84

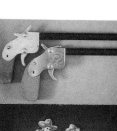

85

77
"ROLLFAST" 3.5x6″ bw ad card by maker of "Hopalong Cassidy Bikes And Skates" c. 1950. $60

78
"ROLLFAST" 65″ long "Hopalong Cassidy Cowboy Bike" c. 1950. BOY'S VERSION $2,500, GIRL'S VERSION $1,800

79
"AUTOMATIC TELEVISION SET" 5x5x5″ boxed plastic wind-up with paper strips that turn on cylinder to pass behind TV screen. By Automatic Toy Co. c. 1950. BOXED $175, LOOSE $100

80
"HOPALONG CASSIDY" 9.5x19″ boxed Milton Bradley board game © 1950. $75

81
"PONY EXPRESS TOSS GAME" 12x18″ masonite target board with two beanbags by Transogram © 1950. $60

82
"HOPALONG CANASTA" 5.5x8.5x4″ deep boxed game featuring revolving plastic saddle tray plus two card decks and "Hoppy" score pad by Pacific Playing Card Co. © 1950. $250

83
"LASSO GAME" 12.5x15.5″ boxed set of plastic Hoppy on Topper target figure, rope toss rings, color photo. By Transogram © 1950. $150

84
"CHINESE CHECKERS" 12.5x14.5″ boxed set of marbles and playing board in printed design of "Sheriff" badge. By Milton Bradley © 1950. $75

85
"BAR TWENTY SHOOTING GAME" 10x15″ boxed set of die-cut cardboard target figures and pair of 11.5″ metal/wood pistols for firing rubber bands. By Chad Valley Co., England, © 1953. $250

86
HOPPY 9x14x3″ boxed set of black leather belt and double holster holding pair of gold finished metal cap guns with black plastic grips c. early 1950s. BOXED $800, LOOSE $500

87
''AUTHENTIC SHOOT 'N IRON'' 4x9.5″ boxed Australian cap gun c. early 1950s. $175

88
''HOP A' LONG'' 30″ long tin clicker rifle with color decal by Marx Toys c. early 1950s. $300

89
HOPPY 4x8x2″ boxed 8″ black plastic ''Pistol Flashlight'' that lights by pulling trigger c. early 1950s. BOXED $200, LOOSE $100

90
HOPPY 9.5″ long silvered metal cap gun with black plastic grips, each with raised portrait in white. By Schmidt Mfg. Co. c. early 1950s. $250

91
HOPPY 9″ long silvered metal cap pistol with ivory plastic grips, each with etched portrait. By Wyandotte Co. c. early 1950s. $150

92
HOPPY 7.5″ long silvered metal cap pistol with ivory plastic grips, each with name in rope script c. early 1950s. $100

93
HOPPY 7″ brass finished metal cap pistol with black plastic grips, each with name spelled in white rope script c. early 1950s. $100

94
HOPPY 9″ gold finished metal cap pistol with black plastic grips, each with etched portrait. Belt and holster are black leather c. early 1950s. HOLSTER $150, GUN $200

95
HOPPY black leather belt and holster set designed to fit pair of 9″ cap guns c. early 1950s. $200

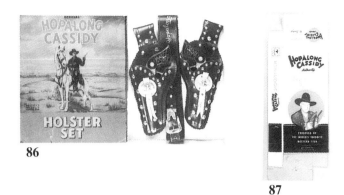

86 **87**

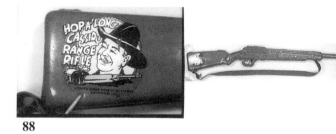

88

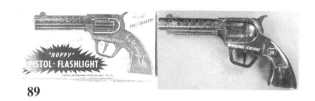

89

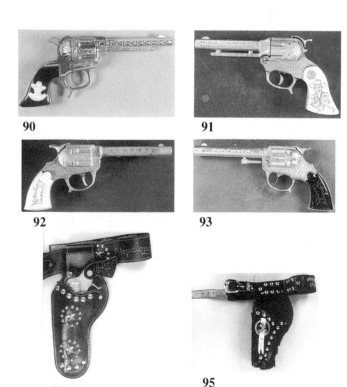

90 **91**

92 **93**

94 **95**

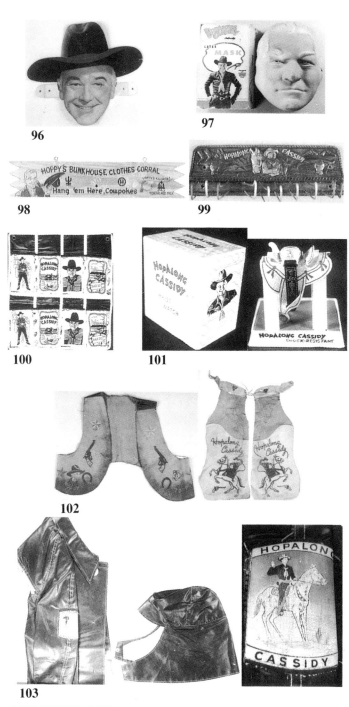

96

97

98

99

100

101

102

103

104

96
HOPPY 11″ tall by 13″ wide color paper mask with ad on back for endorsed pudding c. 1950. $100

97
HOPPY 5x8.5x2″ boxed latex mask c. 1950. BOXED $200, LOOSE $100

98
''BUNKHOUSE CLOTHES CORRAL'' 4.5x23.5″ wide wooden hanger with extended clothing pegs. Right end has stamped name of local sponsor c. 1950. $150

99
HOPPY 4x11.5″ wide composition wood hanger with extended metal holders for neckties c. 1950. $100

100
HOPPY 14.5x15.5″ vinyl hanger with eight pockets for holding child's shoes or slippers c. 1950. $100

101
HOPPY 3x4x4.5″ boxed wristwatch on cardboard saddle display stand © 1950. BOXED $300, LOOSE $50

102
HOPPY suede leather chaps and matching vest from child's cowboy outfit c. early 1950s. $200

103
HOPPY child's black rubberized raincoat and hat with color patch on each arm of the coat c. early 1950s. $175

104
HOPPY 11x14x2″ boxed girl's fabric jacket and skirt outfit accented by vinyl picture panels c. 1951. BOXED $175, LOOSE $75

105
HOPPY black felt hat with chin cord that has leather "Bar 20 Deputy" adjustment slide c. 1950. $150

106
HOPPY & TOPPER 6.5" tall wool winter cap by Pedigree Sportswear c. 1950. $75

107
HOPPY child's fabric brim cap with color portrait c. 1950. $75

108
HOPPY black leather gloves with name and art inked in white c. 1950. $100

109
HOPPY ON TOPPER 12x12" handkerchief with tin steer head tie slide c. 1950. $125

110
HOPPY ON TOPPER 13" long pre-tied child's necktie c. early 1950s. $75

111
HOPPY & TOPPER 36" long fabric neckerchief with silver plastic tie slide c. 1950. $75

112
HOPPY dark cotton twill trousers by Blue Bell c. 1950. $150

113
HOPPY woven fabric child's sweater c. 1950. $150

114
HOPPY boy's underwear briefs with various Hoppy and Topper scenes c. 1950. $150

115
HOPPY 7x10x4" deep boxed set of child's bw leather boots by Acme Co. © 1951. BOXED $400, LOOSE $200

105

106

107

108

109

110

111

112

113

114

115

117

116

118   **119**

120   **121**

122

123

124

125

126

127   **128**   **129**

116
HOPPY 4.25x8.25x2.5″ boxed leather wrist cuffs c. 1950. BOXED $250, LOOSE $100

117
HOPPY 5.5x7.5″ carded fabric hair bow c. 1950. $85

118
HOPPY & TOPPER 4x4.5″ black zipper billfold c. 1950. $75

119
HOPPY 3.5x4.5″ brown leather zipper billfold c. 1950. $75

120
HOPPY 5x13″ carded leather belt by Yale Belt Corp. c. 1950. CARDED $300, LOOSE $100

121
HOPPY 9″ long display box holding sterling silver identification bracelet. By Anson c. 1950. BOXED $150, LOOSE $75

122
HOPPY 3.25x4″ carded 2″ ''Hopalong Cassidy'' silvered brass star badge c. 1950. CARDED $75, LOOSE $35

123
HOPPY 6″ ballpoint pen with refill cylinder in box c. 1950. PEN $75, REFILL $25

124
''CRAYON AND STENCIL'' 9.5x11.5x1.5″ boxed set by Transogram © 1950. $150

125
''COLORING OUTFIT'' 12x15.5x1.5″ boxed set by Transogram © 1950. $150

126
HOPPY 10.5x14″ canvas school book bag c. 1950. $150

127
HOPPY 4x8″ cardboard holster holding plastic gun pencil case c. 1950. $150

128
HOPPY 4.5x8.5x1.5″ stiff cardboard pencil case c. 1950. $125

129
''WILLIAM BOYD'' 8x10″ school tablet c. 1950. $30

130
HOPPY 9.5x12.5x1.5″ boxed set of three jigsaw puzzles by Milton Bradley c. 1950. $100

131
HOPPY 11.25x15″ frame tray inlay jigsaw puzzle © 1950. $40

132
HOPPY 9x11.5″ frame tray inlay jigsaw puzzle by Whitman © 1950. $30

133
HOPPY 14.5x23x21″ tall padded vinyl and chromed metal tubing child's TV rocker chair by Comfort Lines c. 1950. $300

134
HOPPY 6.5″ metal flashlight with color decal plus Morse Code listing on barrel c. 1950. $75

135
HOPPY RADIO in 4x5.5x8.25″ wide metal case with embossed foil portrait in two versions by Arvin Industries c. 1950. TOPPER FRONT LEGS DOWN $200, LEGS UP (SEE FRONT COVER) $300

136
HOPPY 5″ dia. by 5.5″ tall metal case key-wind alarm clock by U.S. Time c. 1950. $300

137
HOPPY 3.5″ steel pocketknife with bw plastic picture panel on both sides c. 1950. $75

138
HOPPY 26″ wide rolled fabric sleeping bag c. 1950. $250

139
HOPPY 24x60″ chenille fabric throw rug c. 1950. $100

140
HOPPY 18.5″ wide wallpaper strip c. 1950. $125

141
HOPPY 35x70″ fabric remnant c. 1950. $100

142
''HAIR TRAINER'' 5.25″ tall 4-oz. bottle of hair oil also issued in larger size c. 1950. THIS SIZE $35, QUART SIZE $90

130 **131** **132**

133 **134**

135 **136** **137**

138 **139**

140 **141** **142**

143

144

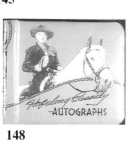

145

146   **147**

148   **149**

150   **151**   **152**

153   **154**

155

156

143
"DR. WEST'S DENTAL KIT"
8x9x1.5″ boxed set of toothbrush,
boxed toothpaste tube, Hoppy portrait mirror c. 1950. $200

144
"BAR 20 RIDES AGAIN"
4x4x1″ boxed 16mm home movie
film c. 1950. $30

145
"HEART OF THE WEST"
5x8x1.5″ boxed set of six film-
strips for use in included plastic
film viewer c. 1950. $200

146
HOPPY 4.5x4.5″ View-Master
stereo reel #955 © 1950. $10

147
HOPPY 4.5x4.5″ View-Master
stereo reel #956 © 1953. $15

148
"AUTOGRAPHS" 5x6″ vinyl
covered rigid book zippered on
three sides c. 1950. $150

149
HOPPY 10.25x13.75″ vinyl covered scrapbook c. 1950. $125

150
HOPPY 18x19″ high gloss color
fabric pillow cover c. 1950. $75

151
HOPPY 18x19″ high gloss color
fabric pillow cover c. 1950. $75

152
HOPPY 6.5″ dia. by 11″ tall ceramic "Cookie Barrel" with saddle design lid c. 1950. $500

153
HOPPY 8″ dia. by 6″ tall ceramic
"Cookie Corral" c. 1950. $400

154
HOPPY 6x8″ Wheaties box back
panel including "Trail Dust"
movie title c. 1936. $85

155
HOPPY 5x9x3″ deep "Hopalong
Cassidy Candy Bar" box by Ryan
Candy Co. © 1950. $200

156
"HOPALONG CASSIDY" 5x6″
foil candy bar wrapper from box
#155 © 1950. $100

157
"HOPALONG CASSIDY COOK-
IES" 2x5x8" tall box by Burry's
Co. © 1950. $400

158
"HOPALONG CASSIDY'S
SUGAR CONES" 2x5x8" tall box
with Hoppy art on all panels except bottom c. 1950. $600

159
"HOPALONG CASSIDY PO-
TATO CHIPS" 7.5" dia. by 11.5"
tall tin with lid c. 1950. $200

160
HOPPY 9" tall waxed cardboard
local milk carton with Hoppy art
on one panel c. 1950. $125

161
"DAIRYLEA DAIRY PROD-
UCTS" 3.5x6.75" closed premium
folder sheet offering six Hoppy
premiums c. 1950. $100

162
"DAIRYLEA" 7" long cardboard
click gun premium by same sponsor as #161 c. 1950. $100

163
"COTTAGE CHEESE" 4.5" dia.
12-oz. container with tin lid c.
1950. $25

164
"SUNBEAM BREAD" 3.5x5.5"
sales sample color card with back
offer for same picture in poster
size c. 1950. $35

165
HOPPY 11x15.5" cardboard sign
with area for name of "Special
Guest" on TV show sponsored by
Wonder Bread c. 1950. $175

166
"GRAPE NUTS FLAKES"
8.5x11" handbill imprinted for local distribution as probable gro-
cery bag insert c. 1950. $150

167
"BOND BREAD" 12x18" stiff
paper book cover c. 1950. $30

168
"BOND BREAD" 3.5x7" pre-
mium comic booklet with story
"The Strange Legacy" © 1951.
$30

157

158

159

160

161

162

163

164

165

166

167

168

169

170

171

172

173

174

175

176

177

178

179

169
''BOND BREAD'' 5.5x7″ diecut rigid cardboard store hanger sign c. 1950. $250

170
''BOND BREAD'' 10.25x13.5″ window display card with local imprint c. 1950. $150

171
''BOND BREAD'' 3.5x5.5″ premium card c. 1950. $25

172
''BOND BREAD'' 2x3″ card from series offering bread labels c. 1950. EACH $10

173
''BOND BREAD'' 8.5x15″ closed folder for mounting second series of bread labels numbered 33-48 c. 1950. $150

174
HOPPY 7x8x3.5″ deep red or blue steel lunch box with front color decal in irregular outline. Issued with 6.5″ steel bottle by Aladdin Industries © 1950. BOX $125, BOTTLE $60

175
''HEALTHY PALS!'' 3″ tall white bathroom glass with ''Mornin' Pards!'' on reverse c. 1950. $75

176
HOPPY 7x8x3.5″ deep red or blue steel lunch box with front color decal in rectangle outline. Issued with 6.5″ tall steel bottle by Aladdin Industries © 1952. BOX $140, BOTTLE $60

177
''WESTERN SERIES'' 4.75″ tall clear glass tumbler with color art for ''Cowboy Branding Irons'' from set of at least four c. 1950. EACH $50

178
HOPPY 7x8x4″ deep steel lunch box with 6.5″ steel bottle by Aladdin Industries © 1954. BOX $250, BOTTLE $90

179
HOPPY 3″ tall white glass milk mug from set of four, each with different art in different single color c. 1950. EACH $20

180
HOPPY 5″ tall set of three white glass tumblers for milk at breakfast, lunch and dinner c. 1950. EACH $30

180

181
"BAR 20 CHOW SET" 4.5x4.5x7″ boxed white glass plate, bowl and tumbler for "Gun Totin' Buckaroos" c. 1950. BOXED $250, EACH LOOSE $50

181

182
HOPPY chinaware set of 9.5″ plate, 5.25″ dia. bowl, 3″ mug c. 1950. EACH PIECE $75

182

183
HOPPY chinaware set of 9.5″ plate, 5.25″ dia. bowl, 3″ mug c. 1950. EACH PIECE $65

183

184
"SAVINGS CLUB" 9x12″ enveloped "Hoppy Thrift Kit" of letter, certificate, fold-out leaflet, color photo c. 1951. $150, PHOTO ALONE $25

185
HOPPY 1.25″ green/bw celluloid button with metal hanger c. 1950. $30, NO HANGER $20

186
HOPPY 1.25″ green/bw celluloid button with metal hanger c. 1950. $30, NO HANGER $20

187
"SAVINGS CLUB" 3″ bwr litho tin button worn by bank tellers c. 1951. $75 (SEE NOTE ON PAGE 6 ABOUT REPRODUCTIONS)

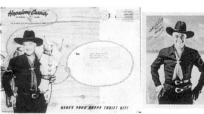
184

185

186

187

How The West Was Won

An epic western family TV series, based loosely on the 1962 movie of the same title with a star-studded cast including Gregory Peck, Henry Fonda, James Stewart, Debbie Reynolds, George Peppard. The TV version piloted January 19, 1976 as a made-for-TV movie titled *The Macahans*. A 1977 sequel, followed by the 1978-79 series, were both retitled *How The West Was Won*. The series starred James Arness, previously of *Gunsmoke*, as Zeb Macahan, leader of the Macahan family clan during its trial-fraught journey westward in the Civil War era.

1

2

3

4

5

6

7

8

9

1
''ZEB MACAHAN'' 2x8x10.5″ tall boxed action figure with outfit and accessories by Mattel © 1978. $35

2
''HOW THE WEST WAS WON'' 3.5x11x18″ boxed plastic playset by Timpo © 1977. $40

3
''HOW THE WEST WAS WON'' 6.5x11″ carded ''Log Cabin Attack'' plastic set by Fleetwood © 1978. $15

4
''HOW THE WEST WAS WON'' 2x8x11.5″ boxed set of simulated leather holster and 8″ metal cap pistol by Nichols Co. © 1978. $75

5
''HOW THE WEST WAS WON'' 5.5x11″ carded plastic knife and sheath set by Nichols Co. c. 1978. $20

6
''HOW THE WEST WAS WON'' 8x10x1.5″ boxed jigsaw puzzle by HG Toys © 1978. $12

7
''HOW THE WEST WAS WON'' 8x10.5x1.5″ boxed jigsaw puzzle by HG Toys © 1978. $12

8
''HOW THE WEST WAS WON'' 6.5″ plastic bottle by King-Seeley Co. $20

9
''HOW THE WEST WAS WON'' 6.5x8.5x4″ deep steel lunch box by King-Seeley Co. © 1976. $30

Johnny Mack Brown (1904–1974)

All-American football halfback at University of Alabama, striking good looks, plus movie roles opposite leading screen actresses such as Joan Crawford, Norma Shearer, Mary Pickford, Marion Davies, Greta Garbo, Mae West—all preceded the beginning of Johnny Mack Brown's prolific career of cowboy movies. His first starring western role was in the 1930 release *Billy The Kid*, a sound version still noted for its use of a 70mm process called Grandeur Screen. He is credited with at least 130 western films; other sources claim he starred in more than 200 westerns including those destroyed by a studio fire of the late 1940s. He still appeared in cameo western roles as late as 1966.

1
"GUN TALK" 27x41" movie poster of 1947. $50

2
WHEATIES BOX 6x8" clipped back panel including movie title "Lawless Land" of 1937. $35

3
"RIDERS OF PASCO BASIN" 2.25" Dixie Ice Cream lid with 1940 title. $20

4
"LAW MEN" 2.25" Dixie Ice Cream lid. 1944 title. $15

5
"JOHNNY MACK BROWN" 8x10" Dixie Ice Cream color picture of 1943. $25

6
"JOHNNY MACK BROWN" 8x10" Dixie Ice Cream picture with 1943 movie title. $25

7
BROWN-HATTON 8x10" Dixie Ice Cream picture with Raymond Hatton and title for 1948 movie. $20

8
"WILD WEST DAYS" 2.5x3.5" bw card from set of 12 based on 1937 movie. SET $75

9
JOHNNY MACK BROWN 5x7" bw photo with personal salutation added in pencil above facsimile signature c. early 1950s. $35

10
"JOHNNY MACK BROWN" 11x14" Saalfield coloring book © 1952. $35

11
"JOHNNY MACK BROWN" 7.5x10" Dell comic book #7 for October-November 1951. $15

1

2

3

4

5

6

7

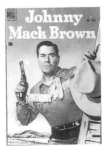
8

9

10

11

John Wayne (1907–1979)

"Duke," an actor of imposing stature, both physcially and as a leading man in action films for nearly a half century. Prior to his film career, Wayne was an outstanding football player at University of Southern California. In an interview shortly before his death, he credited Howard Jones, his football coach and close friend of Tom Mix, with opening the door to film work. After several bit parts beginning in 1928, his first significant role was in the 1930 epic of that era, *The Big Trail*. His career never ceased thereafter until his final screen appearance in a 1976 western, *The Shootist*. In all, Wayne appeared in more than 150 films, including about 85 of western nature. His portrayal of Rooster Cogburn in *True Grit* earned him his first Academy Award Oscar in the twilight of his career.

1

2

3   5

6   7

8

9   10   11

1
"SHE WORE A YELLOW RIBBON" 11x14″ color lobby card #7 from set for 1949 movie. $75

2
TINTED PAPER PHOTO 5×7″ also picturing horse "Duke" c. 1930s. $25

3
JOHN WAYNE 3.5x5.5″ tinted bw English card c. 1930s. $40

4
"THREE MESQUITEERS" 8x10″ publicity photo of Wayne, Max Terhune, Ray Corrigan with ad on back for movie "Santa Fe Stampede" of 1938. $50

5
JOHN WAYNE 3.5x5.5″ sepia card from English "Picturegoer" series c. 1930s. $25

6
"KING OF THE PECOS" 2.25″ Dixie Ice Cream waxed cardboard cup lid with 1936 movie title. $30

7
"THE QUIET MAN" 2.75″ Dixie Ice Cream lid with title of 1952 non-western movie. $15

8
JOHN WAYNE 8x10″ Dixie Ice Cream picture titled on back for "King Of The Pecos" 1936. $85

9
JOHN WAYNE 3.5x5.5″ English "Film Partners" card also picturing Claire Trevor c. 1930s. $20

10
AUTOGRAPHED 8x10″ bw photo signed in 1977. $250

11
"TIME" 8.25x11″ weekly magazine for March 3, 1952. $15

12
"LIFE" 10.5x13.5" weekly magazine issue for May 7, 1965. $15

13
"WESTWARD HO!" 4x5.5" Engle-Van Wiseman movie storybook © 1935. $60

14
"THE SHEPHERD OF THE HILLS" 5.5x7.5" Grosset & Dunlap book 1941. $20

15
JOHN WAYNE 11x14" Saalfield coloring book © 1951. $100

16
SAALFIELD 11x15.5" coloring book with pack of "John Wayne Crayon Ranch House" crayons attached on front © 1951. $100

17
"JOHN WAYNE ADVENTURE ANNUAL" 8.5x11.5" English book © 1958. $40

18
JOHN WAYNE 3x7" premium comic offered by Oxydol and Dreft soaps. 1950. $45

19
"EL DORADO" 7.5x10" Dell comic book 1967. $40

20
"IN OLD OKLAHOMA" 9x12" sheet music with cover art including Dale Evans © 1943. $75

21
"THE ALAMO" 45 rpm Golden Record © 1960. $25

22
JOHN WAYNE 10x11x3" boxed set of leather belt and double holsters c. early 1950s. BOXED $350, LOOSE $150

23
SAALFIELD 11.5x15" frame tray puzzle © 1951. $75

24
"JOHN 'DUKE' WAYNE" 7.25" memoriam plate c. 1979. $35

25
MEMORIAM 3.5" rwb/bw celluloid badge 1979. $10

12

13

14

15

16

17

18

19

20

21

22

23

24

25

Ken Maynard (1895–1973)

Self-described as "just a good ol' cowpoke," Maynard nevertheless was an extremely accomplished horseman, probably the first actual singing cowboy, and one of the best-known western idols from the mid-1920s through early 1940s. Maynard slid into a film saddle easily from experiences as a rider in touring Wild West shows, Barnum & Bailey Circus and others after leaving his Texas ranch boyhood. He appeared in more than 80 films between 1925 and 1944, ably supported in most by Tarzan, his "Wonder Horse." His younger brother Kermit was also an established star of western and adventure films.

1

2

3

4

5

6

7

8

9

10

11

1
"LIGHTNING STRIKES WEST"
12x18″ press book for 1940 Colony Pictures film. $30

2
"WHISTLIN' DAN" 8x11″ re-release press book for re-issued 1932 movie. $20

3
AUTOGRAPHED "KEN MAYNARD" 8x10″ photo signed 1941. $150

4
"GLORIOUS TRAIL" 3.5x5.5″ gum card c. 1930s. $12

5
MAYNARD-BUZZ BARTON 3.5x5.5″ exhibit card © 1921. $15

6
KEN MAYNARD 3.5x5.5″ exhibit card c. 1930s. $10

7
KEN MAYNARD 8x10″ Dixie Ice Cream picture c. early 1930s. $50

8
KEN MAYNARD 8x10″ Dixie Ice Cream picture 1934. $40

9
KEN MAYNARD 8x10″ Dixie Ice Cream picture 1934. $30

10
KEN MAYNARD 8x10″ Dixie Ice Cream picture 1934. $30

11
KEN MAYNARD 3.5x5.5″ English postcard c. 1934. $20

12
''SIX-GUN LAW'' 2.5x3.5″
Whitman penny book © 1938.
$20

13
KEN MAYNARD 3.5x4.5″ Whitman Better Little Book © 1939.
$40

14
''WHEELS OF DESTINY''
4x5.5″ Engel-Van Wiseman movie
book © 1934. $50

15
''WESTERN FRONTIER'' 4x5.5″
Lynn book © 1935. $40

16
KEN MAYNARD 7.5x10″ Faw-
cett British comic book #3
© 1950. $65

17
KEN MAYNARD 9x12″ song folio © 1935. $35

18
''THE STRAWBERRY ROAN''
9x12″ sheet music © 1931. $25

19
KEN MAYNARD 1x3″ paper cigar band c. 1930s. $25

20
''BUCKAROO CLUB''
2.25x4.25″ radio club card c.
1930s. $75

21
''COLE BROS. CIRCUS''
8.5x11.5″ program c. 1938. $50

22
''COLE BROS. CIRCUS'' 17x17″
bandanna c. 1938. $100

23
KEN MAYNARD cowboy cos-
tume of bandanna, chaps and
matching shirt c. 1930s. COM-
PLETE $175

12

13

14

15

16

17

18

19

20

21

22

23

Laramie

An hour-long TV series about the difficulties of two brothers in operating a combination cattle ranch and stagecoach station near Laramie in the 1870s Wyoming Territory. The brothers, Slim and Andy Sherman, were portrayed respectively by John Smith and Bobby Crawford Jr. Veteran song composer Hoagy Carmichael was featured as Jonesy, the chief ranch hand during the show's first season. Robert Fuller was featured as a drifter who settled in as ranch partner. The show aired from September 15, 1959 to September 17, 1963 on NBC.

1

2

3

4

1
TV GUIDE 5x7.5″ issue for week of April 23, 1960. $10

2
''JOHN SMITH'' 3.5x5.5″ sepia postcard from English ''Picture-goer'' series c. early 1960s. $12

3
''JOHN SMITH'' 3.5x5.5″ sepia postcard from English ''Picture-goer'' series c. early 1960s. $12

4
''JOHN SMITH'' 3.25x5″ bw card #309 from set of 64 titled ''TV Western Stars'' by Nu Trading Cards c. 1960s. $3

5
''LARAMIE ANNUAL'' 8.25x11″ English book © 1961. $30

6
''LARAMIE FROM THE TELE-VISION SERIES'' 8.25x11″ English book © 1964. $25

7
''LARAMIE FROM THE TELE-VISION SERIES'' 8.25x11″ English book © 1965. $25

8
''LARAMIE'' 9x17.5″ boxed board game by Lowell Toy © 1960. $60

9
''LARAMIE'' 10″ lithographed tin gun for firing cork c. early 1960s. $35

5

6

7

8

9

Lash La Rue (b. 1917)

The "King of the Bullwhip" western star who used this weapon and quick six-shooters to bring villains to justice for about a decade. He was introduced as the character "Cheyenne Kid" in his first western, *Song Of Old Wyoming,* in 1945. Studio publicists were responsible for his instruction with the black bullwhip and substituted the new nickname "Lash" for his actual first name of Alfred. His outfit remained the same stern black throughout the La Rue series. He suffered (or benefitted) throughout his career by comparison to Humphrey Bogart due to remarkable facial likeness. In the early 1950s, he performed extensively in traveling rodeos, carnivals and other personal appearances.

1
"CHEYENNE TAKES OVER"
27x41″ movie poster of 1947. $75

2
"CHEYENNE TAKES OVER"
22x26″ movie poster of 1947. $50

3
"PIONEER JUSTICE" 11x17″
movie pressbook of 1947. $30

4
AUTOGRAPHED "LASH LA
RUE" 11x14″ "Outlaw Country"
movie lobby card of 1949. $75

5
"THE THUNDERING TRAIL"
11x14″ movie lobby card of 1951.
$25

6
LASH LA RUE 3.5x5.5″ bw exhibit card c. early 1950s. $15

7
LASH LA RUE 11x14″ bw fan
photo c. early 1950s. $40

8
AUTOGRAPHED "LASH LA
RUE" 8x10″ bw photo c. 1949.
$75

9
"LASH LA RUE WESTERN"
7.5x10″ comic book of October
1950. $35

10
"SIX-GUN HEROES" 7.5x10″
comic book of June 1952. $40

11
"THE VANISHING OUTPOST"
7x10.25″ "Motion Picture
Comic" of July 1952. $85

2

1

3

4

5

6

7

8

9

10

11

Lawman

A half-hour TV series starring steely-eyed John Russell as stern, no-nonsense Marshal Dan Troop of Laramie, Wyoming during the 1870s. His assistant deputy was quick-gunned Johnny McKay played by Peter Brown. The series by Warner Bros. aired on ABC October 5, 1958 to October 2, 1962.

1

2

3

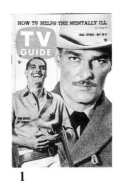

4

5

6

7

8

9

10

11

12

1
TV GUIDE 5x7.5″ issue for week of July 25, 1959. $12

2
"LAWMAN COWPUNCHER BOOTS" 14.5x24″ cardboard easel store sign c. 1960. $350

3
JOHN RUSSELL 3.5x5.5″ color postcard c. 1960. $15

4
AUTOGRAPHED 8x10″ bw photo c. 1960s. $30

5
"PICTUREGOER" 3.5x5.5″ sepia English postcard c. 1960. $15

6
"TV AND MOVIE WESTERN" magazine of Oct. 1959. $50

7
LAWMAN 3.25x5″ bw card #101 from set of 64 titled "TV Western Stars" by Nu Trading Cards c. 1960s. $3

8
JOHN RUSSELL/LAWMAN 8″ tall replica figure by Hartland Plastics Co. c. early 1960s. BOXED $250, LOOSE $150

9
"JOHNNY McKAY" boxed 8″ tall replica figure by Hartland Plastics Co. c. early 1960s. BOXED $300, LOOSE $200

10
LAWMAN 24″ long cloth and leather chaps c. 1960. $35

11
LAWMAN 3x8x8″ boxed "Cowpuncher Boots" c. 1960. $100

12
LAWMAN 6.5x8.5x4″ deep steel lunch box with bottle by King-Seeley Co. © 1961. BOX $125, BOTTLE (NOT SHOWN) $50

The Life and Legend of Wyatt Earp

Movie re-creations of the life of actual lawman Earp began shortly after his death in 1929. Prior to his death, he had recounted his life story to author Stuart Lake and published it in 1931 as *Wyatt Earp: Frontier Marshal*. Frontier Marshal film versions were released in 1934 and 1939, the latter starring Randolph Scott. Among the actors portraying Earp in later film versions under various titles were Richard Dix (1942), Henry Fonda (1946), Joel McCrea (1955), Burt Lancaster (1957), Guy Madison in a European version circa 1960. The popular TV series starred Hugh O'Brian and aired on ABC from September 6, 1955 to September 26, 1961. Virtually all licensed Earp collectibles are from the TV era.

1
TV GUIDE 5x7.5″ issue for February 9, 1957. $15

2
TV GUIDE 5x7.5″ issue for April 12, 1958. $12

3 TV GUIDE 5x7.5″ issue for May 2, 1959. $12

4
''HUGH O'BRIAN'' 8.5x11″ booklet by TV sponsors General Mills, Procter & Gamble 1967. $35

5
''TV WESTERN ROUNDUP'' 8.5x11″ Vol. 1 #1 magazine 1957. $50

6
WYATT EARP 4.5x5.75″ Whitman Big Little Book #1644 © 1958. $18

7
WYATT EARP 11x14″ Saalfield coloring book © 1957. $30

8
WYATT EARP 8.5x11″ Whitman coloring book © 1958. $20

9
WYATT EARP 8.5x11″ Watkins-Strathmore coloring book © 1958. $25

10
WYATT EARP 8.5x11″ Giant Fun Time cut-out coloring book © 1958. $35

11
WYATT EARP 7x7″ RCA Victor single 45 rpm record album c. late 1950s. $20

12
WYATT EARP 2x4.25x11.75″ boxed Pyro Plastics assembly kit for 10″ figure c. 1958. $75

1

2

3

4

5

6

7

8

9

10

11

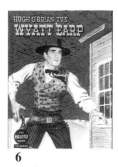

12

13

14

15

16

17

18

19

20

21

22

13
WYATT EARP 3x8.5x9.5″ boxed Hartland Plastics full sized figure c. late 1950s. BOXED $250, LOOSE $100

14
WYATT EARP 8″ tall Hartland Plastics figure c. late 1950s. BOXED $250, LOOSE $150

15
WYATT EARP 7x11.5″ carded Hartland Plastics © 1960. CARDED $80, LOOSE $40

16
''HUGH O'BRIAN/WYATT EARP/DODGE CITY WESTERN TOWN'' 3x10x35″ boxed Marx Toys playset c. late 1950s. $600

17
WYATT EARP 2x9x17.5″ boxed Transogram game © 1958. Example shows lid and spinners. $60

18
WYATT EARP ''PEACE-MAKER'' 7.5x10″ Cheerios box with back panel ad c. late 1950s. $125

19
WYATT EARP ''BUNTLINE SPECIAL'' 18″ long black plastic clicker gun on 6x20″ card c. late 1950s. CARDED $150, LOOSE $75

20
WYATT EARP ''BUNTLINE SPECIAL'' 11″ long silvered metal cap gun on 5.5x12″ card by Hubley Co. © 1959. CARDED $125, LOOSE $25

21
''JUNIOR WYATT EARP'' 9x10″ carded double gun and holster set by Hubley Co. © 1959. $150

22
WYATT EARP ''BUNTLINE SPECIAL'' 6x11″ carded silvered metal cap gun c. late 1950s. CARDED $125, LOOSE $25

23
WYATT EARP 2.5x11.5x14″ boxed set of leather holsters and metal cap guns c. late 1950s. BOXED $175, LOOSE $75

24
WYATT EARP 3x11x12″ boxed "Marshal's Outfit" of fabric outfit, vinyl holsters, plastic clicker guns, metal badge © 1957. $75

25
WYATT EARP "BUNTLINE SPECIAL" 7.5x15″ full color newspaper ad 1957. $15

26
WYATT EARP "BUNTLINE SPECIAL" 1x3x9″ boxed 9″ silvered metal cap pistol by Crescent Toys of England c. early 1960s. BOXED $125, LOOSE $75

27
"WYATT EARP" 9.5″ long leather/cardboard holster set on matching belt c. late 1950s. $40

28
"MARSHAL WYATT EARP" 3x4″ vinyl wallet © 1957. $25

29
WYATT EARP 1.25x10x11″ boxed Transogram crayon and stencil set © 1958. $60

30
WYATT EARP 2x7x9″ boxed Whitman jigsaw puzzle c. late 1950s. $20

31
WYATT EARP 11x14″ Whitman frame tray inlay jigsaw puzzle c. late 1950s. $20

32
"HUGH O'BRIAN AS WYATT EARP" 8x10″ school tablet c. late 1950s. $20

33
WYATT EARP 3x4″ carded 2″ metal "Marshal" badge c. 1960. CARDED $25, LOOSE $15

34
WYATT EARP 2.5″ tall by 5″ dia. glass cereal bowl c. 1960. $25

23

24

25

26

27

28

29

30

31

32

33

34

The Lone Ranger

The Lone Ranger began his journey into western lore from a radio station in Detroit on a Monday evening, January 30, 1933. The evening premiered a new adventure series, hopefully to appeal to both children and adults, based fictionally on the actual exploits of late 19th century Texas Rangers with likely a touch of folk hero Zorro added in. It was soon made obvious that the Lone Ranger, a champion of justice, was masked—hitherto mostly the prerogative of robbers and bandits. The story concept, developed by WXYZ station owner George Trendle assisted by a promising writer named Fran Striker, quickly soared into series popularity due to linked broadcasts with major stations WGN, Chicago, and WOR, New York City. The all-important radio voice of the Lone Ranger passed from Jack Deeds to George Seaton and finally to Earle Graser in May of 1933. Graser's auto death in 1941 was followed smoothly in voice transition by Brace Beemer who continued in the role throughout the radio series until its demise in 1955. *The Lone Ranger* 15-chapter movie serial by Republic Pictures began in 1938. Lee Powell portrayed the masked mystery man. A sequel serial one year later, *The Lone Ranger Rides Again*, introduced Robert Livingston in the lead role. The TV series beginning in 1949 added Clayton Moore to the well-traveled title role, only to be replaced briefly by John Hart, and then reinstated for the remainder of the series, ending in 1957. Two full-length Lone Ranger movies were released in 1956 and 1957 under Wrather Productions, both starring Moore plus Jay Silverheels as Tonto. A Saturday morning TV cartoon version began September 10, 1966 and lasted three years. In 1980 a TV cartoon series by Filmation joined the Lone Ranger with another yesteryear idol, Tarzan. This series concluded in about two years. The most recent movie release was the 1981 Wrather production *The Legend of the Lone Ranger*.

1

1

3

4

5

6   7   8

1
"THE LONE RANGER" 11x14" lobby card 1938. $60

2
"THE LONE RANGER RIDES AGAIN" 11x14" lobby card 1939. $60

3
"THE LONE RANGER AND THE LOST CITY OF GOLD" 11x17" pressbook 1958. $75

4
LONE RANGER/SGT. PRESTON 14x22" poster for circus performance c. 1960s. $150

5
LONE RANGER 17.5x21.5" poster for Lone Ranger family restaurant chain c. early 1970s. $25

6
"LEE POWELL" 3.5x5.5" exhibit card c. late 1930s. $12

7
"CHIEF THUNDERCLOUD" 3.5x5.5" exhibit card picturing him as Tonto c. late 1930s. $12

8
"THE FIVE RANGERS" 3.5x5.5" exhibit card c. late 1930s. $12

9
AUTOGRAPHED ''CLAYTON MOORE'' 8x10″ bw photo signed c. 1970s. $40

10
AUTOGRAPHED ''TONTO'' 8x10″ photo of Jay Silverheels 1950s. $75

11
LONE RANGER 3.5x6″ short-wave radio operator's card c. 1950s. $25

12
''RADIO GUIDE'' 10.5x13.5″ schedule listing magazine of September 17, 1938. $40

13
ZEMBO TEMPLE SHRINE CIRCUS 9x11.5″ program for April 1959. $35

14
''TV WESTERN AND MOVIE'' 8x11″ magazine for June 1959. $50

15
LONE RANGER 9.5x14″ Warner Bros. promotional book for first feature length film c. 1956. $200

16
LONE RANGER 4x5.5″ Fast-Action Story book © 1938. $75

17
LONE RANGER 3.5x4.5″ Whitman Big Little Book © 1935. $35

18
LONE RANGER 3.5x4.5″ Whitman Big Little Book © 1936. $40

19
LONE RANGER 3.5x4.5″ Whitman Better Little Book © 1939. $50

20
LONE RANGER 3.5x4.5″ Whitman Better Little Book © 1942. $50

21
LONE RANGER 3.5x4.5″ Whitman Better Little Book © 1943. $50

9

10

11

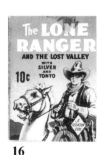

12

13

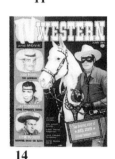

14

15

16   **17**   **18**

19   **20**   **21**

22

23

24

25

26

27

28

29

30

31

32

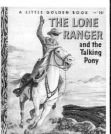

33

34

35

36

22-24
LONE RANGER 5.5x7.5″ hard-cover books published and re-printed by Grosset & Dunlap from 1930s through 1950s in at least 15-numbered series. First printings with dust jackets EACH $25, re-prints with dust jacket EACH $15

25
LONE RANGER 11x14″ Whitman coloring book © 1938. $75

26
LONE RANGER 8.5x11.5″ Whit-man coloring book © 1941. $60

27
LONE RANGER 1x8x8.5″ boxed set of six Whitman coloring books © 1955. $40

28
HI-YO SILVER 6.5x7.5″ Whit-man coloring book © 1955. $20

29
LONE RANGER 8x11″ Western Publishing Co. coloring book © 1975. $15

30
TONTO 8.5x11″ Whitman color-ing book © 1955. $30

31
LONE RANGER 8.5x11.5″ Dell Publishing Co. book © 1938. $100

32
LONE RANGER 7x10″ Grosset & Dunlap book © 1938. $100

33
LONE RANGER 11x15.5″ scrap-book by unidentified publisher c. 1940s. $50

34
LONE RANGER 6.75x8″ Little Golden Book © 1958. $15

35
LONE RANGER 10x13.5″ scrap-book by Whitman c. 1950s. $25

36
LONE RANGER 8.5x9.5″ Ran-dom House diecut book © 1981. $10

37
"LONE RANGER COMICS"
7.5x10.5" first issue premium
booklet by Lone Ranger Ice
Cream Cones 1938-1939. $800

38
"LONE RANGER'S WESTERN
TREASURY" 7.5x10" first issue
Dell Giants comic book for Sep-
tember 1953. $100

39
"LONE RANGER MOVIE
STORY" 7.5x10" Dell Giant
Comic for 1956. $175

40
LONE RANGER 6.75x8.25" Dell
Publishing Co. folder sheet that
opens to 8.25x33.5" with five full
color illustrations © 1951. Example photo shows three pictures
from folder. $100

41
LONE RANGER 6.25x19.5" original comic strip art by Charles
Flanders for publication December
19, 1959. $125

42
LONE RANGER 10x10" individ-
ually enveloped and numbered set
of eight Decca Records in 78 rpm
size, also issued in 45 rpm size,
both © 1951 or 1952. Either size
EACH $25

43
LONE RANGER 3.5x13x35" tall
pressed wood guitar by Superior
Musical Instruments c. 1940s.
$150

44
LONE RANGER 4.25" wide plastic harmonica on 4x4.5" diecut
card c. 1950s. PACKAGED $50,
LOOSE $20

45
TONTO 4.5" dia. by 6" tall metal
drum with rubber drum heads plus
wood drumsticks c. 1950s. $75

37   **38**

40

39

41

42

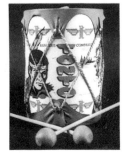

43   **44**   **45**

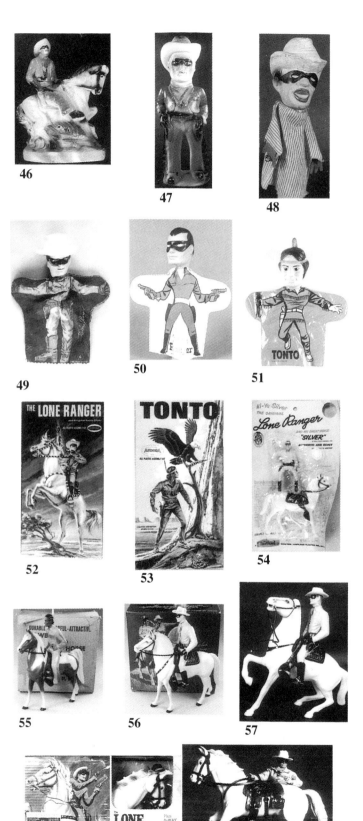

46

47

48

49

50

51

52

53

54

55

56

57

58

46
LONE RANGER 11″ tall plaster carnival statue c. 1940s. $100

47
LONE RANGER 15″ tall plaster carnival statue c. 1940s. $60

48
LONE RANGER 11″ tall hand puppet-early 1950s. $125

49
LONE RANGER 10″ tall hand puppet c. 1950s. $30

50
LONE RANGER 11″ tall hand puppet © 1966. $25

51
TONTO 11″ tall hand puppet © 1966. $25

52
LONE RANGER & SILVER 2x7x13″ boxed model assembly kit by Aurora Plastics © 1967. $150

53
TONTO 2x7x13″ boxed model assembly kit by Aurora Plastics © 1967. $150

54
LONE RANGER & SILVER 7x11.5″ carded small size figures by Hartland Plastics © 1960. CARDED $100, LOOSE $40

55
TONTO & SCOUT 3x8.5x9.5″ boxed large size figures by Hartland Plastics © 1954. BOXED $250, LOOSE $100

56
LONE RANGER & SILVER 3x8.5x9.5″ boxed large size figures by Hartland Plastics © 1954. BOXED $250, LOOSE $175

57
LONE RANGER & SILVER 3x8.5x9.5″ boxed figures by Hartland Plastics c. late 1950s. BOXED $250, LOOSE $150

58
LONE RANGER & SILVER 4.5x9.5x16″ boxed plastic jointed action figure with accessories by Gabriel Industries © 1977. BOXED $75, LOOSE $35

59
LONE RANGER 7″ tall lithographed tin wind-up by Marx Toys © 1938 with box. METALLIC SILVER FINISH $350, WHITE PAINT FINISH $275, IF BOXED ADD $200

60
''LONE RANGER/RANGE RIDER'' 2.5x9.5x11″ wide litho tin wind-up by Marx Toys using original 1938 figure on new litho tin rocker base that has additional ''Range Rider'' title. c. 1950s reissue. $250

61
''HI-YO SILVER'' 10.5x21″ tall by 36″ long painted wood rocking horse c. 1940s. $250

62
''LONE RANGER RODEO'' 3x13x15″ boxed playset by Marx Toys c. 1950. $200

63
LONE RANGER 2x10x19″ boxed Parker Brothers board game © 1938. $50

64
LONE RANGER 1x3.5x5″ boxed Parker Brothers card game © 1938. $40

65
LONE RANGER 16x27″ full color litho tin target by Marx Toys © 1938. $100

66
LONE RANGER 1.5x17.5x17.5″ boxed 17″ dia. full color cardboard target by Marx Toys © 1946. BOXED $150, LOOSE $85

67 ''LONE RANGER AND THE SILVER BULLETS'' 2x13.5x16″ boxed board game © 1956. $75

68
LONE RANGER 1.5x5.5x10.5″ boxed cardboard simulated leather holster and 7″ aluminum cap gun © 1942. BOXED $200, LOOSE $100

59

60

61

62

63

64

65

66

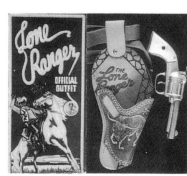

67

68

69

70

71

72

73

74

75

76

77

69
LONE RANGER 1.5x5x10″ boxed 10″ long leather gun holster and belt set with black horsehair accent on holster c. 1939. BOXED $150, LOOSE $75

70
LONE RANGER 1x4x9″ boxed 9″ long cast iron cap gun with ''Shel-Glo'' white plastic grips by Hubley c. late 1940s. BOXED $250, LOOSE $150

71
LONE RANGER 4x13.5x16″ cardboard carrying case holding leather double holster and belt, nickel plated cast iron cap guns, set of metal spurs, leather spur guards and wrist cuffs by Esquire Novelty Co. c. 1950s. $500

72
LONE RANGER 1.5x4x10″ boxed 9″ long plastic ''Smoking Click Pistol'' by Marx Toys c. 1950s. BOXED $200, LOOSE $125

73
LONE RANGER 11″ long set of metal ''Fanner 50'' cap guns with plastic grips, each in black rubber belt and double holster set by Mattel Toys c. late 1950s. $75

74
LONE RANGER 6x9.5″ carded plastic gun in vinyl holster plus metal hand cuffs and star badge inscribed ''Lone Ranger Deputy'' by 20th Century Varieties © 1966. $40

75
LONE RANGER .5x3.5x4″ boxed pocketwatch with miniature metal gun and leather holster strap fob by New Haven Clock Co. © 1940. BOXED $450, WATCH $300

76
LONE RANGER 2″ dia. pocketwatch by New Haven Time Co. © 1939. $300

77
LONE RANGER ⅞″ dial face wristwatch with silvered metal bezel and original brown leather straps c. 1951. $150

78
LONE RANGER 1x1.5″ tin case
toy watch with simulated leather
straps c. 1950s. $75

79
LONE RANGER 4x10x11″ boxed
pair of leather western boots with
Lone Ranger title on elastic boot
straps. By Endicott-Johnson
© 1948. BOXED $200, LOOSE
$100

80
LONE RANGER 1x9x11″ boxed
set of three jigsaw puzzles by Puzzle Craft Industries © 1945. Third
puzzle is similar to box lid design.
$175

81
LONE RANGER 11.5x14.5″
Whitman frame tray inlay jigsaw
puzzle c. 1970s. $10

82
LONE RANGER 4″ dia. by 5.5″
tall canister holding jigsaw puzzle
c. 1970s. $20

83
LONE RANGER 9.5x13″ frame
tray inlay jigsaw puzzle © 1978.
$15

84
LONE RANGER 1x5.5x8.5″
boxed picture printing set with
rubber stamps, stamp pad and
booklet by Stamperkraft © 1939.
$100

85
LONE RANGER .5x4.5x5.5″
litho tin case holding paint set by
Milton Bradley c. 1950s. $25

86
LONE RANGER 10.5x12″ vinyl
and fabric school bag with shoul-
der strap c. 1950s. $125

87
LONE RANGER 9x14″ canvas
fabric school bag with plastic handle c. 1950s. $100

78

79

80

81 **82** **83**

84 **85**

86 **87**

88

89

90

91

92

93

94

95

96

97

98

88
LONE RANGER 4″ tall painted composition toothbrush holder on 1.25x2″ base © 1938. $75

89
LONE RANGER 2x2x5″ boxed hair brush © 1939. BOXED $85, LOOSE $50

90
LONE RANGER 1x3x3.5″ tall metal bank © 1938. $90

91
LONE RANGER 1.5x4x6″ litho tin case holding First Aid Kit by White Cross Labs © 1938. $25

92
LONE RANGER 5x7″ First Aid Guide and Western lore booklet from First Aid Kit by White Cross Labs © 1938. $85

93
LONE RANGER 6x8x14″ wide brown bakelite plastic electrical radio by ''Pilot,'' also made in ivory color bakelite case, c. late 1930s. $1000

94
LONE RANGER 5x6x7.5″ wide white plastic electrical radio by ''Majestic'' c. 1950s. $1000

95
LONE RANGER 6x10x12.5″ wide wooden case record player by Decca c. late 1940s-early 1950s. $175

96
LONE RANGER 1x3.5x5.5″ box containing leather belt attachment that holds three ''Silver Bullet'' pens c. 1941. $125

97
LONE RANGER 3.25x4″ brown vinyl wallet with color cover art c. 1953. $85

98
LONE RANGER & TONTO 3.5x13x22″ boxed ''Lone Ranger And Tonto Wigwam'' child's play tent of canvas cloth. Underside of box has cut-out masks and accessories. © 1958. $150

99
LONE RANGER 2x2x7″ boxed
6.5″ Flashlight mid-1950s.
BOXED $100, LOOSE $50

100
LONE RANGER 3″ long pocketknife 1950s. $100

101
LONE RANGER 7x11″ carded
"Chuck Wagon Gong" 1950s.
$100

102
LONE RANGER 7x9″ carded
viewer © 1955. $40

103
LONE RANGER 4.5x4.5″ View-
Master set © 1956. $30

104
LONE RANGER 4.5x4.5″ View-
Master set © 1981. $15

105
LONE RANGER 5″ tall glass
tumbler © 1938. $100

106
LONE RANGER 6″ long silver
plate brass spoon picturing Lone
Ranger on Silver at handle tip
© 1938. $50

107
CHEERIOS 2.5x6.5x8.5″ tall cereal box with bw cut-out back
panel from coloring contest series
c. 1951. $150

108
LONE RANGER 6.5x8.5x3.5″
deep flat steel lunch box by
ADCO Liberty c. 1954. RED
SIDES VERSION $300, BLUE
SIDES $400

109
LONE RANGER 7x8x4″ deep embossed steel lunch box with 6.5″
bottle by Aladdin Industries
© 1980. BOX $30, BOTTLE $15

110
"LONE RANGER TARGET
GAME" 9x10.5″ folded stiff paper punch-out sheet that opens
to three panels holding targets
and gun to be fired by rubber
band. Morton's Salt © 1938.
UNPUNCHED $350

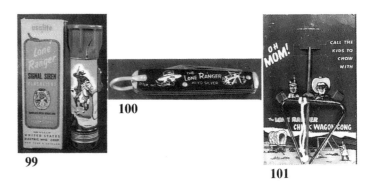

99

100

101

102

103

104

105

106

107

108

109

110

111   **112**   **113**

114   **115**

LONE RANGER

COBAKCO

116   **117**   **118**

119   **120**   **121**

111
LONE RANGER 3.5x5.5″ card by radio sponsor Silver Cup Bread including call letters of one of original pilot radio stations, WGN (Chicago) 1934. $50

112
LONE RANGER 8x10.5″ paper sheet premium for radio sponsor VBEV beverage c. late 1930s. $50

113
LONE RANGER 4x6.5″ premium card by Silver Cup Bread 1938. $50

114
LONE RANGER 3.5x5.5″ bw photo card by Silver Cup Bread listing radio air times on reverse c. late 1930s. $40

115
LONE RANGER 4.5x10″ diecut cardboard "Bat-O-Ball" paddle with attached rubber band and rubber ball. © 1939. $150

116
LONE RANGER 11x14″ two-sided cardboard poster and 1″ enameled brass pin COBAKCO Bread mid-1930s. POSTER $350, PIN $50.

117
LONE RANGER 3.75x6″ bw card by COBAKCO Bread c. mid-1930s. $100

118
"CHUCK LIVINGSTON" 4x6.25″ bw photo card of the "Outlaw Lone Ranger Dramas" by COBAKCO Bread c. mid-1930s. $75

119
"LONE RANGER SAFETY CLUB" 8x15″ calendar by Merita Bread for 1950. $400

120
LONE RANGER 8x10″ bw photo by Merita Bread 1940s. $120

121
LONE RANGER 8x12″ diecut cardboard store hanger sign for Bond Bread © 1940. $350

122
LONE RANGER 1.5″ metal star badge and 3.25x5.5″ mailing envelope from Safety Club of Bond Bread c. 1938-1940. PACKAGED $100, LOOSE $50

123
LONE RANGER 2.75″ dia. aluminum pedometer with cloth strap in 1x3x3″ mailing carton from Cheerios c. 1948. BOXED $100, LOOSE $50

124
LONE RANGER 21.5x22.5″ rwb fabric bandanna premium by Cheerios c. 1949-1950. $60

125
LONE RANGER & TONTO 8x10″ color photo 1950s. $20

126
LONE RANGER 1.25x3x4″ mailing box holding ''Movie Film Ring'' with instruction slip and filmstrip offered as Cheerios premium 1949-1950. INSTRUCTIONS $35, FILMSTRIP $100, RING $65

127
''LONE RANGER 6-SHOOTER RING'' 17x22″ full color paper poster by Kix cereal 1948. $150

128
LONE RANGER 10x11″ carded 12 metal badges 1950s. CARD $75, BADGE $25

129
''LONE RANGER DEPUTY'' 2.25″ silvered metal star badge also depicting mask on 3.5x4″ card © 1966. $40

130
LONE RANGER 1x2.5x9″ boxed four sets of 30 for 120 total cards by Ed-U-Cards c. 1950s. BOXED SET, EACH $150, INDIVIDUAL CARDS, EACH $4

131
LONE RANGER 1.5x3.25″ ''Tattoo Transfers'' c. 1970s. EACH $8

122

123

124

125

126

127   **128**   **129**

130

131

Maverick

Light humor TV series starring James Garner as Bret Maverick, a dapper journeyman poker player who preferably avoided other types of western conflicts. He was joined early in the series by Jack Kelly as brother Bart Maverick. The series began September 22, 1957 and continued to July 8, 1962, although Garner departed his role in 1960. Practically all collectibles are from the Garner era rather than the final years of the original run that introduced Beauregard Maverick (Roger Moore) and finally Brent Maverick (Robert Colbert).

1

2

3

4

5

6

7

8

9

10

11

12

1
TV GUIDE 5x7.5″ issue for November 9, 1957. $20

2
TV GUIDE 5x7.5″ issue for March 17, 1959. $15

3
TV GUIDE 5x7.5″ issue for September 5, 1959. $15

4
AUTOGRAPHED ''JAMES GARNER'' 8x10″ glossy bw photo c. late 1950s. $50

5
MAVERICK 6x7″ bw photo late 1950s. $30

6
MAVERICK ''SCOUT-O-RAMA'' 8x10.5″ closed mailing folder previewing James Garner appearances at Boy Scout event held in San Francisco 1958. $35

7
JAMES GARNER 3.5x5.5″ full color fan card c. 1959. $20

8
JAMES GARNER 3.5x5.5″ sepia photo postcard from English ''Picturegoer'' series e. late 1950s. $15

9
JACK KELLY 3.5x5.5″ sepia photo postcard from English ''Picturegoer'' series c. late 1950s. $15

10
JAMES GARNER 3.5x5.5″ bw photo card late 1950s. $15

11
JACK KELLY 3.25x5″ bw card #2 from set of 64 titled ''TV Western Stars'' by Nu Trading Cards c. 1960s. $3

12
JAMES GARNER 3.25x5″ bw card #114 from set #11. $3

13
"POKER ACCORDING TO MAVERICK" 4.25x6.5" Dell paperback © 1959. $12

14
MAVERICK 6x8" Whitman hardcover book © 1959. $15

15
"TV WESTERN AND MOVIE" 8.5x11" magazine for December 1958. $50

16
MAVERICK 7x9.5" "Eras-O Picture Book" with crayons © 1960. $50

17
MAVERICK 7.5x10" Dell comic book #16 for 1961. $25

18
MAVERICK 7.5x10.25" English hardcover © 1960. $45

19
MAVERICK 7.25x10" English hardcover © 1961. $30

20
MAVERICK 8.5x12" English hardcover © 1961. $30

21
MAVERICK 7.25x10" English hardcover © 1962. $30

22
MAVERICK 6x8" enveloped Little Golden Record © 1958. $15

23
BRET MAVERICK 3x8.5x9.5" boxed full size figure by Hartland Plastics c. late 1950s. BOXED $300, LOOSE $200

24
BRET MAVERICK 8" tall James Garner figure by Hartland Plastics c. late 1950s. BOXED $300, LOOSE $200

25
MAVERICK 3x4" vinyl wallet © 1958. $30

26
MAVERICK 2x3.5" vinyl key case keychain holder with bw photo cover and inside notepad c. late 1950s. $25

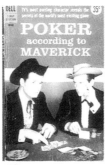
13

14

15

16

17

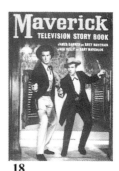
18

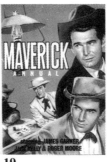
19

20

21

22

23

24

25

26

27

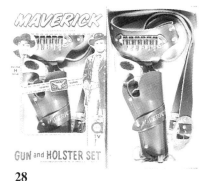

28

29

30

31

32

33

34

27
MAVERICK 1.25x4.5x27″ boxed 27″ long plastic clicker "Saddle Rifle" by Marx Toys c. late 1950s. BOXED $250, LOOSE $100

28
MAVERICK 2x9x14.5″ boxed 10.5″ silvered metal cap pistol with ivory plastic grips in brown leather holster belt set by Leslie-Henry Co. © 1958. BOXED $400, LOOSE $150

29
MAVERICK 6x9.5″ carded 4.5″ long metal single shot cap pistol in vinyl wrist holster. Card pictures James Garner c. late 1950s. CARDED $100, LOOSE $50

30
MAVERICK 12x13x3.5″ tall woven straw cowboy hat with fabric label on crown picturing James Garner © 1958. $40

31
MAVERICK 3x5″ carded 3.5″ long silvered metal "Hide-A-Way Derringer" single shot cap pistol with plastic grips by Leslie-Henry Co. c. late 1950s. CARDED $60, LOOSE $20

32
MAVERICK 4x7″ diecut card picturing James Garner as Bret Maverick holding clip-on string tie with metal clasp © 1959. $35

33
MAVERICK 4x7″ diecut card picturing Jack Kelly as Bart Maverick holding clip-on string tie with metal clasp © 1959. $35

34
MAVERICK 4.5″ dia. plastic canteen holding diecut metal badge inserted by paper picture of James Garner c. late 1950s. $35

The Range Rider

Early TV series produced by Gene Autry Flying A Productions starring gangly Jock Mahoney in the title role. He was ably assisted in his 1860s freelance law enforcement heroics by young sidekick Dick West played by Dick Jones. Both were accomplished western stuntmen, a skill used frequently throughout the series. The show premiered April 26, 1951 and was initially syndicated for regional and local sponsors. Later network distribution carried it into the mid-1960s.

1
''JOCK MAHONEY'' 8x10″ school tablet c. 1950s. $25

2
TV GUIDE 5x8.25″ full color photo of Dick Jones and Jock Mahoney from ''TV Guide Cowboy Album'' series and this particular photo appeared in Pittsburgh Tri-State Edition for August 14, 1953. $15

3
RANGE RIDER 8x10″ bw photo with facsimile signatures plus back premium ad for Langendorf Bread c. early 1950s. $25

4
RANGE RIDER 13x16″ sales promotion kit folder c. 1950s. $50

5
RANGE RIDER 11x12.25″ Abbott Publishing Co. coloring book with 16 pages © 1956. $35

6
''THE FLYING A'S RANGE RIDER'' 7.5x10″ Dell comic book #10 for June-August 1955. $18

7
RANGE RIDER 5.5x8.5″ closed folder that opens to 11x17″ for mounting 16 bread loaf wrapper labels issued as set by ButterKrust Bread c. mid-1950s. $75

8
RANGE RIDER 1.5x6.5x9.5″ boxed jigsaw puzzle by Gabriel Toys © 1955. $30

1

2

3

4

5

6

7

8

Rawhide

TV series based on the problems and perils encountered during a sprawling cattle drive from Texas to stockyards in Kansas and Missouri. Co-stars were Eric Fleming as Gil Favor, the trail boss, and Clint Eastwood as Rowdy Yates, the drive's ramrod and troubleshooter. The series premiered January 9, 1959 and continued until January 4, 1966. Eastwood became trail boss in the final year following the departure of Fleming from the role. The series theme song was popularized by vocalist Frankie Laine.

1

2

3

4

5

6

7

8

9   10

1
TV GUIDE 5x7.5″ issue for February 4, 1961. $20

2
"TV-MOVIE-WESTERN" 8.5x11″ magazine for March 1960. $50

3
AUTOGRAPHED "CLINT EASTWOOD" 8x10″ full color photo c. early 1960s. $65

4
"RAWHIDE ANNUAL" 7x10″ English hardcover © 1960. $75

5
"RAWHIDE" 8.5x11″ English hardcover book © 1960. $85

6
"RAWHIDE" 8.25x11″ English hardcover book © 1961. $85

7
RAWHIDE 3x8.5x9.5″ boxed full size Gil Favor figure by Hartland Plastics c. early 1960s. BOXED $400, LOOSE $300

8
"RAWHIDE" 2x9x17.5″ boxed Lowell Toy board game © 1960. $65

9
"RAWHIDE" 1.5x2.5″ tan leather keychain holster holding miniature metal six-shooter with simulated pearl plastic grips early 1960s. $35

10
"RAWHIDE" 28″ long vinyl and fabric chaps and matching vest sized accordingly early 1960s. $50

The Rebel

TV series drawing its name from an ex-Confederate soldier of the Civil War who roamed the west searching for post-war employment, often complicated by his insistent wearing of a Confederate cap. The title role of Johnny Yuma starred Nick Adams throughout the October 4, 1959 to September 17, 1961 run of the series. The show's theme song *Johnny Yuma,* sung by Johnny Cash, became a moderately successful record in its own right.

1
NICK ADAMS AS REBEL 8x10″ bw illustration for use in Strength & Health Magazine c. 1960. $25

2
NICK ADAMS 8x10″ bw photo, also picturing former heavyweight boxing champion Joe Louis and unidentified weightlifter for use in Strength & Health Magazine c. 1960. $20

3
NICK ADAMS 3.25x5″ bw card #311 from set of 64 titled "TV Western Stars" by Nu Trading Cards c. 1960s. $3

4
"THE REBEL" 6x8″ Whitman hardcover book © 1961. $25

5
"JOHNNY YUMA/THE REBEL" 7x11.5″ carded small size figure and horse by Hartland Plastics. Example photo shows in-correct horse as original issue is dark color with raised foreleg. c. early 1960s. CARDED $125, LOOSE $75

6
"THE REBEL" 2x16.5x19″ boxed Ideal Toy board game © 1961. $85

7
"THE REBEL" 21″ long tin toy rifle with varnished wood stock that has "Rebel" art on left side. Gun has cocking mechanism for producing pop sound. Japanese made c. early 1960s. $150

1   **2**   **3**

4   **5**

6

7

Red Ryder

A popular name in western action lore, both from the print version created by Fred Harman and several movie versions based on the Harman character and his youthful Indian sidekick, Little Beaver. *Red Ryder* first emerged in Sunday comic strip form November 6, 1938 although essentially a re-named adventurer from Harman's earlier *Bronc Peeler* strip. The strip became daily in 1939 and the 1940s began the movie versions starring, among others, Bill Elliott, Red Barry, Rocky Lane. Bobby Blake was the movie version Little Beaver followed by Tommy Cook. Concurrently a radio version began in 1942 and continued through the decade. Most Red Ryder collectibles are based on the illustrated character including the long-run association with Daisy Air Rifle advertising.

1

2

3

4

5

6

7

8

9

10

1
RED RYDER 22x28″ poster from movie series starring Jim Bannon c. early 1950s. $30

2
BILL ELLIOTT/BOBBY BLAKE 8x10″ Dixie picture c. 1946. $40

3
BOBBY BLAKE 8x10″ Dixie picture c. 1945. $40

4
RED RYDER & LITTLE BEAVER 3.5x5.5″ bw fan card with facsimile signatures c. 1940s. $50

5
RED RYDER 3.5x4.5″ Whitman Better Little Book © 1939. $35

6
RED RYDER 3.5x4.5″ Whitman Better Little Book © 1946. $30

7
RED RYDER 3.5x4.5″ Whitman Better Little Book © 1948. $30

8
RED RYDER 3.25x5.5″ Whitman Better Little Book © 1949. $25

9
RED RYDER 8.5x11″ Whitman coloring book © 1952. $30

10
LITTLE BEAVER 8x11″ Whitman coloring book © 1956. $25

11
LITTLE BEAVER 8.5x11″ Whitman coloring book © 1955. $30

12
RED RYDER 5.5x8″ Whitman hardcover book © 1956. $20

13
RED RYDER 5.5x8″ Whitman hardcover book © 1951. $20

14
RED RYDER 3x4″ Whitman Penny Book © 1939. $30

15
"DAISY GUN BOOK" 4.5x5.25″ catalogue of products by Daisy Mfg. Co. © 1955. $75

16
"DAISY AIR RIFLES" 6x9″ catalogue of toy guns also for Superman, Buck Jones, Buck Rogers © 1940. $125

17
RED RYDER 2x12x16″ boxed "Whirli-Crow Game" of cork-firing rifle and crow targets on rigid wires by Daisy Mfg. Co. c. 1940s. $100

18
RED RYDER 2x5x13″ boxed "Pop-Um Shooting Game" with similar contents to #17 by Daisy Mfg. Co. c. 1940s. $100

19
RED RYDER 2x10x13″ boxed target game with standup target for wooden balls by Whitman © 1939. $100

20
"RED RYDER CORRAL" 9x16.5″ metal bagatelle marble game by Gotham Pressed Steel Corp. c. 1940s. $75

11

12

13

14

15

16

17

18

19

20

21

22

23

24

25

26

27

28

29

30   **31**

21
RED RYDER 11x14″ Jaymar frame tray inlay jigsaw puzzle © 1951. $20

22
RED RYDER 9.75x12.5″ Jaymar frame tray inlay jigsaw puzzle c. 1951. $20

23
LITTLE BEAVER 11.5x14.5″ Whitman frame tray inlay jigsaw puzzle © 1956. $20

24
RED RYDER & LITTLE BEAVER 6.5″ metal flashlight © 1949. $40

25
"LITTLE BEAVER ARCHERY SET" 8x31″ stiff cardboard target © 1951. $30

26
RED RYDER 17x24″ cut fabric from larger panel with art in red/green/bw on tan bkg. c. 1950. $50

27
RED RYDER/LITTLE BEAVER/YAQUI JOE 15x30″ cut cloth from larger fabric with art in brown/rwb c. 1950s. $50

28
"RED RYDER VICTORY PATROL" 3.25x3.5″ diecut cardboard badge with art in luminous glow material on red c. early 1940s. $75

29
"RED RYDER VICTORY PATROL" 6.5x15″ rwb paper sign by bread sponsor c. early 1940s. $200

30
RED RYDER 3x11x22″ fiberboard salesman's sample case for glove lines by Wells-Lamont Co. c. early 1950s. $200

31
RED RYDER 6x10″ sheet of trading cards packaged with Wells-Lamont gloves © 1952. UNCUT $75

The Restless Gun

A somewhat similar, but earlier, series to *The Rebel* based on the westward wanderings of Vint Bonner, Civil War veteran and proficient gunfighter when called on. The series starred John Payne, an established film star in other types of roles. The show premiered September 23, 1957 and continued through September 14, 1959.

1
"VERMONT VIDEO GUIDE" 5.25x8.25" issue for October 6, 1957. $20

2
TV GUIDE 5x7.5" issue for January 18, 1958. $15

3
JOHN PAYNE 3.25x5" bw card #312 from set of 64 titled "TV Western Stars" by Nu Trading Cards c. 1960s. $3

4
THE RESTLESS GUN 6x8" Whitman hardcover book © 1959. $20

5
THE RESTLESS GUN 8.5x11" Saalfield coloring book © 1958. $35

6
"TV'S RESTLESS GUN" 2x4.5x11.5" boxed assembly parts for 10" figure by Pyro Plastics c. 1958. $75

7
"VINT BONNER" 2x3x9.5" boxed figure by Hartland Plastics c. late 1950s. BOXED $250, LOOSE $175

8
"RESTLESS GUN" 2x12x15" boxed leather belt and holster with 12 toy bullets and 9" metal cap gun that can convert to longer pistol rifle by Esquire Novelty Corp. © 1958. BOXED $250, LOOSE $125

9
"RESTLESS GUN" 10" long silvered metal cap gun with brown plastic grips and secret compartment in the handle late 1950s. $75

10
THE RESTLESS GUN 2x9.5x19" boxed Milton Bradley board game utilizing marbles © 1959. $40

1 2 3

4 5

6

7 8

9 10

Rex Allen (b. 1922)

Early 1950s film cowboy, known commonly as The Arizona Cowboy from the title of his first film in 1950 which carried on as a nickname through his brief movie career of about five years. Allen picked up the slack left by departure to television of established stars Roy Rogers and Gene Autry. Before filmdom, he was a featured vocalist on a radio barn dance show. He continued to sing in his movies and is generally conceded as the last of the singing cowboys. His career included some 30 films before entering television entertainment himself, principally as the star in a brief 1958 series *Frontier Doctor* as Dr. Bill Baxter.

1

2

3

4

5

6

7

8

9

10

11

1
"SOUTH PACIFIC TRAIL"
27x41" movie poster 1953. $60

2
AUTOGRAPHED "REX AL-
LEN" 8x10" bw photo c. 1960s.
$40

3
REX ALLEN 8x10" bw photo
from radio singing years c. 1945.
$15

4
REX ALLEN 8x10" Dixie picture
with back text for "Arizona Cowboy" movie of 1950. $20

5
REX ALLEN 8x10" Dixie picture
c. early 1950s. $20

6
REX ALLEN & KOKO 8x10"
Dixie picture with back titles of
three films of 1952. $20

7
REX ALLEN 6.25x8.5" back
panel from Quaker Puffed Rice
cereal box from early 1950s set of
eight featuring various western
stars. Panel is #7 with movie title
"Silver City Bonanza" 1951. $20

8
REX ALLEN 2.75" full color
Dixie Ice Cream cup lid with 3-D
viewer ad on back. Movie title is
"Arizona Cowboy" 1950. $40

9
REX ALLEN 9x12" song folio c.
1945. $30

10
REX ALLEN 9x12" song folio
© 1954. $20

11
"COUNTRY SONG ROUNDUP"
8.5x11.5" song folio with Rex Allen cover for February 1954. $15

The Rifleman

Fascinating TV series involving a struggling rancher, Lucas McCain, and his expertise with his Winchester rifle, modified for extremely rapid and continuous firing. McCain (Chuck Conners) was called on weekly to dispense justice by rifle in the somewhat lawless community of North Fork in New Mexico Territory. The typical sub-plot evolved around his motherless son Mark (Johnny Crawford). The series premiered September 30, 1958 and continued through July 1, 1963.

1
TV GUIDE 5x7.5″ issue for March 12, 1960. $25

2
TV GUIDE 5x7.5″ issue for January 20, 1962. $20

3
AUTOGRAPHED ''CHUCK CONNORS'' 4x5″ bw photo c. early 1960s. $35

4
CHUCK CONNORS 3.5x5.5″ bw exhibit card c. early 1960s. $5

5
JOHNNY CRAWFORD & CHUCK CONNORS 3.5x5.5″ bw exhibit card c. early 1960s. $5

6
THE RIFLEMAN 3.25x5″ bw card #116 from set of 64 ''TV Western Stars'' c. 1960s. $3

7
THE RIFLEMAN 5.5x7.75″ Whitman hardcover book © 1959. $25

8
''GUNS'' 8.5x11″ magazine issue for May 1960. $20

9
''CHILDREN'S PLAYMATE MAGAZINE'' 6x9″ for September 1958. $20

10
JOHNNY CRAWFORD 7x7″ enveloped record c. 1959. $20

11
LUCAS McCAIN/RIFLEMAN 3x8.5x9.5″ boxed large size figure by Hartland Plastics c. 1960. BOXED $300, LOOSE $150

12
LUCAS McCAIN/RIFLEMAN 7x11.5″ carded small size figure by Hartland Plastics © 1961. CARDED $100, LOOSE $60

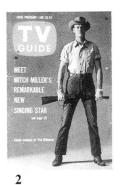

1

2

3

4

5

6

7

8

9

10

11

12

14

13

15

16

17

18

19

20

21

13
THE RIFLEMAN 7.5x10″ Gold Key Comic Book #13 for November 1962. $25

14
THE RIFLEMAN 32″ long metal and plastic replica cap-firing rifle in original box by Hubley Co. © 1958. BOXED $250, LOOSE $150

15
"THE RIFLEMAN RANCH" 4x13x22″ boxed Marx Toys playset c. 1959. $750

16
THE RIFLEMAN 2x10x19″ boxed Milton Bradley board game © 1959. $50

17
THE RIFLEMAN 11x13x3″ tall felt hat with fabric picture label by Tex-Felt © 1958. $75

18
THE RIFLEMAN 7x8x4″ deep flat steel lunch box and 6.5″ steel bottle by Aladdin Industries © 1960. BOX $275, BOTTLE $120

19
THE RIFLEMAN 11.5x14.5″ Whitman frame tray inlay jigsaw puzzle © 1960. $75

20
THE RIFLEMAN 11.5x14.5″ Whitman frame tray inlay jigsaw puzzle © 1960. $60

21
JOHNNY CRAWFORD & CHUCK CONNORS 8x9.5″ school tablet cover c. 1960. $15

Roy Rogers (b. 1911)

"King of the Cowboys," "The Smartest Horse in the Movies," "Queen of the West" are honorary titles thoroughly familiar to all western fans. Roy Rogers, Trigger, and Dale Evans are household names throughout the nation and, indeed, around the world. The success story of Roy Rogers never wavered from his earliest days as cowboy singer Leonard Slye on a remote New Mexico radio station to his phenomenal fan acclaim from movies, radio, recordings, television, personal performances. Len Slye became Dick Weston for about two years before settling on the Roy Rogers name in 1938. About 10 of his earliest film appearances were under the Slye or Weston name. The 1938 Republic feature *Under Western Stars* introduced Roy Rogers to moviegoers and began a career of nearly 100 movie credits. The King of the Cowboys rode easily into even greater success via radio and television. By the mid-1950s he supplanted Hopalong Cassidy as the undisputed "Merchandise King of the Cowboys" as retail items under his endorsement and premium items by sponsors proliferated. The tragic loss of three children within the family evolved into yet another dimension of spiritual and inspirational fandom. Memorabilia from all stages of the Roy Rogers career is avidly sought by thousands of collectors. Thousands of other fans have followed their "Happy Trails" to Roy Rogers' personal museum in Victorville, California.

1
"THE SONS OF THE PI-
ONEERS" 27x41" movie poster
of 1942. $175

2
"UTAH" 27x41" movie poster of
1945. $125

3
"MY PAL TRIGGER" 27x41"
movie poster of 1946. $90

4
"DOWN DAKOTA WAY"
27x41" movie poster of 1949. $75

5
ROY & TRIGGER 8.5x11" full
color laminated wall plaque c.
1950s. $200

6
ROY & TRIGGER 2x5.5' tall full
color poster © 1957. $200

7
"SHINE ON, HARVEST
MOON" 5x7" titled bw photo c.
1938. $25

8
"MANY PLEASANT TRAILS
TO YOU" 8x10" facsimile signa-
ture bw photo c. late 1930s. $35

9
"ROUGH RIDERS ROUND-UP"
2.75" sepia Dixie Ice Cream cup
lid of 1939. $30

1

2

3

4

5

6

7

8

9

10   **11**   **12**

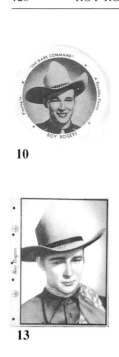

13   **14**   **15**

16   **17**   **18**

19   **20**

21   **22**   **23**

10
"THE DARK COMMAND" 2.5"
Dixie Ice Cream cup lid of 1940.
$30

11
"SONS OF THE PIONEERS"
2.75" Dixie Ice Cream cup lid of
1942. $25

12
"ROY ROGERS" 2.5" Dixie Ice
Cream cup lid c. 1940s. $25

13
ROY 8x10" Dixie Ice Cream picture of 1938. $85

14
ROY & TRIGGER 8x10" Dixie
Ice Cream picture of 1940. $75

15
ROY & TRIGGER 8x10" Dixie
Ice Cream picture c. 1950. $65

16
"HANDS ACROSS THE BOR-
DER" 8x10" Republic Studios
color photo of 1944. $35

17
ROY & TRIGGER 8x10" Quaker
Oats color photo c. 1950s. $30

18
"DOUBLE-R-BAR RANCH"
9x12" fan club newspaper for No-
vember-December 1955. $50

19
"ROY ROGERS FAN CLUB"
3x5" membership card with type-
written date in 1947. $60

20
ROY/DALE FAN CLUB 3x5"
membership card with inked date
in 1956. $30

21
ROY & TRIGGER 5x6" birthday
card by Waldorf Greetings Cards,
England c. 1957. $75

22
ROY & TRIGGER 6.5x8" color
decal sheet © 1952. $40

23
AUTOGRAPHED "HAPPY
TRAILS/ROY ROGERS/TRIG-
GER" 10x10" color portrait illus-
tration c. 1980s. $35

24
"LIFE" 10.5x14″ magazine for July 12, 1943. $25

25
"GRIT" 8x11.5″ magazine story section for June 10, 1945. $35

26
"OUR DOGS-A MAGAZINE FOR DOG LOVERS" 8.25x11″ issue for Winter 1942. $50

27
TV GUIDE 5x7.5″ issue for July 17, 1954. $60

28
"HOLLYWOOD WESTERN" 7.5x11″ magazine for 1950. $40

29
"SCREEN STORIES" 8.5x11″ magazine for July 1950. $30

30
"JET" 4x6″ pocket magazine for February 19, 1953. $75

31
"JACK AND JILL" 7x10″ children's magazine for May 1961. $20

32
"ROY ROGERS RODEO" 8.5x11″ program c. 1948. $75

33
ROY & TRIGGER 8x11″ rodeo souvenir program c. 1950. $40

34
ROY ROGERS 3.5x4.5″ Whitman Better Little Book © 1945. $30

35
ROY ROGERS 3.5x4.5″ Whitman Better Little Book © 1947. $30

36
ROY ROGERS 3.5x4.5″ Whitman Better Little Book © 1949. $25

37
ROY & DALE 10.5x15″ Whitman cut-out dolls book © 1950. UNCUT $125, CUT $50

38
ROY/DALE/DUSTY 10.5x12″ Whitman paperdoll album © 1957. UNCUT $90, CUT $50

24

25

26

27

28

29

30

31
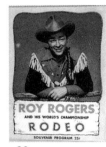
32

33

34
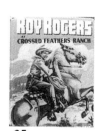
35

36

37

38

39

40

41

43

44

42

45

46

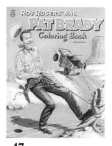

47

48

49

50

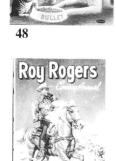

51

52

53

39
ROY ROGERS 6x8″ Whitman book © 1945. $30

40
ROY ROGERS 6x8″ Whitman book © 1946. $30

41
ROY ROGERS 5.5x8″ Whitman book © 1950. $25

42
ROY ROGERS 11x15″ Whitman coloring book © 1948. $60

43
ROY ROGERS 8.5x11″ Whitman coloring book © 1946. $40

44
ROY & DALE 8x11″ Whitman coloring book © 1959. $30

45
DOUBLE-R-BAR RANCH 8x10.5″ Whitman coloring book © 1956. $50

46
ROY & DALE 10.5x11″ Whitman coloring book © 1954. $40

47
PAT BRADY 8.5x11″ Whitman coloring book © 1956. $40

48
TRIGGER/BULLET 8.5x11″ Whitman coloring book 1956. $30

49
BULLET/TRIGGER 7.5x8″ Whitman book 1953. $25

50
"FAVORITE WESTERN STORIES" 1x9x12″ boxed Whitman storybook 1956. BOXED $125, UNBOXED $60

51
"ROY ROGERS COWBOY ANNUAL" 7x10″ English hardcover book © 1957. $50

52
"ROY ROGERS ADVENTURES NO. 1" 8x11″ English hardcover book © 1957. $50

53
"ROY ROGERS ADVENTURES NO. 3" 7x10″ English hardcover book © 1959. $40

54
ROY ROGERS 5.5x6.5″ Whitman Tell-A-Tale book © 1950. $20

55
ROY ROGERS 5.5x6.5″ Whitman Tell-A-Tale book © 1952. $25

56
ROY ROGERS 6.75x8″ Little Golden Book © 1953. $15

57
ROY ROGERS 6.75x8″ Little Golden Book © 1954. $15

58
ROY ROGERS 6.75x8″ Little Golden Book © 1955. $15

59
ROY ROGERS 6.75x8″ Little Golden Book © 1956. $15

60
ROY ROGERS 7.5x10″ Dell comic book #63 from 1945. $145

61
"RIDERS CLUB" 7x10″ premium comic book sent to club members in 1952. $75

62
"RIDERS CLUB" 2.5x4″ membership card c. early 1950s. $40

63
"RIDERS CLUB" 2.25x4″ membership card c. mid-1950s. $35

64
"MARCH OF COMICS" 5x7.5″ retail store premium comic booklet #91 from 1952. $40

65
ROY, DALE & FAMILY 6.5x7.5″ closed paper fold-out that opens to 33″ length with five color photos, three shown in example photo. Subscription premium by Dell Publishing Co. c. early 1950s. $125

54 **55** **56**

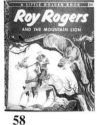
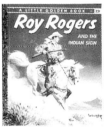

57 **58** **59**

60 **61** **62**

63 **64**

65

66

67

68

69

70

71

72

73

74

75

76

77

66
"SMILES ARE MADE OUT OF THE SUNSHINE" 9x12″ music © 1943. $35

67
ROY ROGERS 9x12″ "Cowboy Songs" folio © 1941. $50

68
ROY ROGERS 9x12″ "Own Songs" folio © 1943. $60

69
"RADIO HIT SONGS" 9x12″ folio 1944. $40

70
"SONGS OF THE SOIL" 10x13″ song folio featuring Roy and five other singing stars © 1948. $50

71
ROY ROGERS 9x12″ song folio © 1952. $30

72
ROY ROGERS 10x10″ "Souvenir Album" holding RCA Victor record of eight songs selected from his movies c. early 1950s. $65

73
"THE MASKED MARAUDER" 7.5x7.5″ enveloped RCA Victor record early 1950s. $50

74
ROY & DALE 7x7.5″ enveloped Little Golden Record c. early 1950s. $20

75
ROY ROGERS 1x1.25x4.5″ boxed metal and plastic "Cowboy Band" harmonica c. 1940s. BOXED $75, LOOSE $30

76
"TEXAS LONG HORN" 11″ long felt pennant suspended from 13″ plastic horn c. 1950s. $100

77
ROY ROGERS 30″ molded stiff cardboard and wood guitar with leaflet in 4x13.5x31″ carton by Range Rhythm Toys c. mid-1950s. BOXED $200, LOOSE $75

78
ROY & TRIGGER 3x8.5x9.5″ boxed full size figures with string tag by Hartland Plastics c. late 1950s. BOXED $250, LOOSE $125

79
ROY & TRIGGER 7x11.5″ carded small size Hartland figures c. 1960. CARDED $100, LOOSE $75

80
BULLET 4″ tall by 6″ long figure scaled to large size Roy and Trigger figures by Hartland Plastics c. late 1950s. BOXED $90, LOOSE $30

81
ROY ROGERS 22″ tall stuffed plush and fabric doll with thin plastic boy's face plus 1.75″ original issue celluloid button by Ideal Toy Co. c. 1950s. DOLL $600, BUTTON $75

82
ROY ROGERS 6.5″ tall composition figure with spring-mounted bobbing head c. 1960s. $125

83
ROY & TRIGGER 3x6x7.5″ tall china bank finished in blended soft colors c. 1949. $150

84
ROY ROGERS 3.5x4x5″ tall metal boot bank in copper finish c. 1950. $40

85
ROY & TRIGGER 2.5″ dia. plastic "Roundup King" yo-yo in cellophane packet by Western Plastics Inc. c. 1950s. $15

86
ROY ROGERS 1x7x14″ boxed set of four hard rubber horseshoes and two tin target bases w/peg for each c. 1950s. BOXED $125, LOOSE $50

78

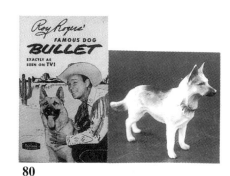

79 **80**

81 **82**

83 **84** **85**

86

87

88

89

90

91

92

93

94

95

96

87
ROY ROGERS "NELLYBELLE" 16x20" tall by 40" long metal pedal car jeep with decal on each side early 1950s. $800

88
ROY ROGERS 4x6x15" boxed plastic horse trailer and jeep with loose figures of Trigger, Roy and Pat Brady by Ideal Toy Co. c. early 1950s. BOXED $300, LOOSE $150

89
"ROY ROGERS WESTERN TOWN" 6x10x34" boxed Marx Toys playset c. early 1950s. $600

90
"ROY ROGERS RODEO" 3.5x13.5x15" boxed Marx Toys playset c. early 1950s. $250

91
"DOUBLE R BAR RANCH" 4x11x24" boxed Marx Toys playset 1950s. $300

92
ROY & TRIGGER 4.5x8.5" tall by 9" long wood and metal musical pull toy that chimes when pulled c. late 1940s. $150

93
ROY ROGERS 7x12" tall by 19" long metal and wood covered wagon pull toy c. late 1940s-early 1950s. $150

94
ROY ROGERS 2x3x7" boxed "Cowboy Branding Iron Set" featuring "RR" miniature branding iron with ink pad c. early 1950s. BOXED $150, LOOSE $75

95
"TRIGGER" 9x18" tall by 19" long stuffed fabric and plush riding toy on metal frame base and wheels c. early 1950s. $200

96
"ROY ROGERS' TRIGGER" 7x18.5" tall by 23" long vinyl and hard plastic riding toy on steel supports and wheels c. early 1950s. $150

97
ROY ROGERS 1.5x5x9″ boxed
"Forty Niner" 9″ cap gun by Les-
lie-Henry Co. c. early 1950s.
BOXED $400, LOOSE $150

97

98
"ROY ROGERS" 2x13x13″
boxed set of leather belt and holsters with 10.5″ cap guns by Classy
Products Corp. © 1956. BOXED
$400, LOOSE $200

99
ROY ROGERS 4.25x4.25″ card
holding "Tuck-A-Way Gun" cap
pistol c. early 1950s. CARDED
$50, LOOSE $20

98   **99**

100
"ROY ROGERS" 2x13x13″
boxed set of leather belt and holsters holding 10.5″ long cap guns
by Classy Products Corp. © 1955.
BOXED $500, LOOSE $300

101
"ROY ROGERS" 2.5″ long plastic gun of puzzle nature for assembly and disassembly, also designed as keychain charm early
1950s. $50

100   **101**

102
ROY ROGERS 1.25x4x8.25″
boxed "Shootin' Iron" 8″ cap pistol by Kilgore Mfg. Co. © 1953.
BOXED $300, LOOSE $125

102

103
ROY ROGERS 1.5x4x10″ boxed
"Shoot'n Iron" 10″ cap pistol by
George Schmidt Co. early 1950s.
BOXED $300, LOOSE $125

103

104
ROY ROGERS 5.5x12.5″ carded
"Shootin' Iron" 8″ generic cap
pistol c. early 1950s. CARDED
$125, LOOSE $50

105
ROY ROGERS 6x10″ carded
"Shootin' Iron" 9.5″ generic cap
pistol c. early 1950s. CARDED
$125, LOOSE $50

106
ROY ROGERS 2x5x26″ boxed
26″ plastic "Cap Shooting Carbine
Rifle" by Marx Toys 1950s.
BOXED $200, LOOSE $100

  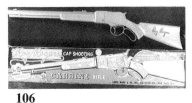

106

104   **105**

107

108

109   **110**

111

112

113

114   **115**

116

107
"ROY ROGERS' RIDERS"
1.5x5.25x7" boxed battery operated "Signal Gun" c. early
1950s. BOXED $250, LOOSE
$150

108
ROY ROGERS 1.75x2.75x4"
boxed wrist watch" by Ingraham
Co. 1951. BOXED $250,
WATCH $150

109
ROY & TRIGGER 2.5x4.5x5"
boxed animated wind-up alarm
clock with name "Roy Rogers &
Trigger" under the alarm dial at
top center of dial face. Small figure of Roy on Trigger rocks back
and forth. By Ingraham Co. c.
1951. BOXED $300, UNBOXED
$200

110
ROY & TRIGGER 1.5x4x4" animated wind-up alarm clock similar
to #109 except this is version that
has no name of Roy and Trigger
on dial face. By Ingraham Co. c.
1951. $150

111
ROY & TRIGGER 2" dia. silvered metal case pocketwatch with
stop watch feature. (Beware of examples with photocopy dial.) By
Bradley Time c. 1959. $400

112
"ROY ROGERS AND TRIG-
GER" 12x12x4" tall woven straw
hat 1950s. $50

113
ROY ROGERS 5x11" card hold-
ing string necktie 1950s.
CARDED $150, LOOSE $50

114
"ROY ROGERS FRONTIER
WEAR" fabric shirt early 1950s.
$75

115
ROY & TRIGGER 17x17" rw fabric bandanna early 1950s. $75

116
ROY ROGERS 1x9x11" boxed
pair of vinyl on fabric "Boot's-
ters." Box bottom has photo
1950s. BOXED $175, LOOSE $75

117
"ROY ROGERS" 8.5" tall pair of child's leather boots with Roy Rogers name also on each elastic pull strap c. 1952. $175

118
"ROY ROGERS" 8" tall pair of child's leather boots c. early 1950s. $125

119
"ROY ROGERS AND TRIGGER" 5" tall pair of child's lined vinyl bedroom slippers early 1950s. $75

120
"ROY ROGERS/TRIGGER" 5x9" pair of child's fabric gloves with vinyl gauntlets and fringe c. early 1950s. $75

121
ROY & TRIGGER 11x14" pebble grained simulated leather schoolbook carrying case c. 1950. $125

122
ROY ROGERS 2.5x8" vinyl pencil case c. early 1950s. $50

123
ROY ROGERS 8x10" school tablet with color cover photo c. early 1950s. $30

124
ROY ROGERS 2.5x4.5" member card for Sears Back-To-School Contest early 1950s. $35

125
ROY ROGERS 1.5x2x6" boxed metal 5" fountain pen 1950s. BOXED $100, LOOSE $50

126
ROY & DALE 1.5x12.5x15.5" boxed "Paint Them Yourself" set of six molded white plaster figures and coloring materials for finishing them. c. early 1950s. $300

127
"ROY ROGERS PAINT SET" 1.5x9.5x13.5" boxed kit of watercolor and crayons plus four picture sheets early 1950s. $150

128
"ROY ROGERS CRAYON SET" 1.5x10x15" boxed kit of art materials and Roy pictures and stencils c. early 1950s. $150

117

118

119

120

121

122

123

124

125

126

127   **128**

129

130

131

132   **133**   **134**

135   136   **137**

138

129
''ROY ROGERS WATER COLOR SET'' 2x11.5x18″ boxed kit of coloring materials and pre-printed picture panels to be finished by numbers. Example photo shows lid and contents plus four completed and framed paintings. c. early 1950s. $150

130
''ROY ROGERS OIL PAINTING SET'' 2x11x15.5″ boxed kit of paint-by-numbers materials c. early 1950s. $150

131
''ROY ROGERS WATER COLOR SET'' 1.5x11.5x16″ boxed kit of paint-by-numbers materials c. early 1950s. $125

132
ROY & TRIGGER 11.5x14.5″ frame tray inlay jigsaw puzzle © 1948. $30

133
ROY & TRIGGER 11.5x13″ frame tray inlay jigsaw puzzle in cardboard cover that indicates puzzle scene © 1950. WITH SLIP COVER $40, WITHOUT $30

134
ROY & PUPPIES 9.5x11.5″ frame tray inlay jigsaw puzzle © 1952. $25

135
ROY ROGERS 2x7x9″ boxed Whitman jigsaw puzzle c. early 1950s. $30

136
ROY/DUSTY/DALE 2x7x9″ boxed Whitman jigsaw puzzle c. early 1950s. $30

137
ROY ROGERS 4x5″ frame tray inlay jigsaw puzzle by Frontiers, Inc. © 1956. $20

138
ROY & TRIGGER 28″ felt pennant c. late 1940s-early 1950s. $75

139
ROY ROGERS 4' tall by 4' dia. base heavy canvas child's tent with accessory poles and ropes c. early 1950s. $150

140
"ROY ROGERS" brown leather pony saddle with tooled Roy art on each hanger panel for stirrup c. late 1940s. $350

141
ROY ROGERS 5x10" packaged "Trick Lasso" with 5.5x9.5" photo showing its use © 1947. PACKAGED $100, LOOSE $30

142
ROY ROGERS 7.5x11" carded and bagged "Trick Lasso" © 1947 but mid-1950s. PACK-AGED $100, LOOSE $30

143
"HAPPY TRAILS/ROY ROG-ERS & TRIGGER" 4.5x9x9.5" hard plastic record player by RCA Victor c. early 1950s. $250

144
ROY ROGERS 3x3.25x4" tall black metal and plastic snapshot camera late 1940s. BOXED $150, LOOSE $75

145
ROY & TRIGGER 8.5" tall (ex-cluding bulb socket) full color painted plaster lamp with 5.5" tall cardboard shade c. 1950s. COM-PLETE $250, NO SHADE $175

146
ROY & TRIGGER 7" long metal and plastic "Signal Siren" flash-light c. early 1950s. $50

147
ROY ROGERS 3" tall metal pocket flashlight with plastic cap c. 1950. $40

148
ROY & DALE 6.5x8.5x3.5" deep flat steel lunch box produced with side panel varieties of wood grain, blue or red by American Thermos 1953-1954. BOX $100, BOTTLE (NOT SHOWN) $50

139

140

141

142

143

144

145

146

147

148

149

150

151

152

153

154

155

156

157

149
ROY & DALE 6.5x9x4″ deep flat steel lunch box by American Thermos c. 1955. BOX $115, BOTTLE (NOT SHOWN) $60

150
ROY & DALE 6.5x8.5x3.5″ deep flat steel lunch box with 8″ steel bottle by American Thermos c. 1957. BOX $125, BOTTLE $60

151
ROY & DALE 4.5x6.5x8.5″ long domed steel ''Chow Wagon'' lunch box by American Thermos c. 1955. BOX $150, BOTTLE (NOT SHOWN) $60

152
ROY ROGERS 7x9x4″ deep lined vinyl lunch box and 8″ tall steel bottle; box is issued in two basic brown and cream colors by King-Seeley Co. c. 1960. BROWN VERSION $150, CREAM VERSION $450, BOTTLE (SAME AS #150) $40

153
TRIGGER 6x8.5x3.5″ deep flat steel lunch box by American Thermos c. 1956. $150

154
''NESTLE'S QUIK'' 3.5x5.5x6″ tall cardboard and tin container for chocolate flavor drink powder with panel ads for Roy Rogers 3-D plastic plaque set. Premium order coupon has expiration date June 30, 1960. $200

155
''ROY ROGERS COOKIES'' 2.25x5.5x7.75″ tall box for Quaker Oats product c. 1948. $300

156
ROY & TRIGGER chinaware set of 9.5″ and 6″ plates, 7″ cereal bowl, 5.25″ dessert dish marked ''Rodeo By Universal'' c. early 1950s. LARGE PLATE $75, OTHERS EACH $40

157
ROY ROGERS 2.75″ dia. by 5″ tall lithographed tin soda can by Continental Beverage Corp, California, c. 1950s. $200

158
ROY ROGERS 1x3.75x3.75″ boxed 16mm film 1950s. $75

159
ROY ROGERS 4.5x4.5″ set of View-Master reels © 1956. $40

160
ROY ROGERS 4x5.5″ Tru-Vue card mid-1950s. $25

161
ROY & TRIGGER 2.5x3.5″ packaged set of ''Trader Cards'' and 1.25″ button c. 1950. PACKAGED SET $400

162
POST CEREAL 2.5x3.25″ ''Pop-Out'' card from set of 36 issued 1952-1955. EACH UNPUNCHED $15

163
KANE PRODUCTS 1.5x2.5″ English set of 25 color photo cards c. 1950s. SET $100

164
POST SUGAR CRISP 2.75x4.25″ 3-D photo folder from 1953-1955 series. EACH $20

165
''ROY ROGERS BUBBLE GUM'' 1.75x2.5″ English set of 24 cards c. 1951. SET $100

166
QUAKER OATS 8.5x11″ order sheet, mailing box and ''Branding Iron'' ring c. 1951. BOX AND LEAFLET $50, RING $125

167
POST CEREAL 2.5″ wide lithographed tin set of 12 rings 1953-1955. EACH $20

168
ROY ROGERS 1.25″ button 1950s. $50

169
ROY & TRIGGER 1.75″ button early 1950s. $30

170
''ROY ROGERS DEPUTY'' 2.5″ tin star badge c. 1950. $20

171
ROY ROGERS 4.5″ tall plastic portrait mug by Quaker Cereals c. 1950. $25

158

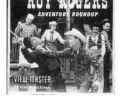

159

160

161

162

163

164

165

166

167

168

169

170

171

Sky King

Early 1950s TV series distinguished by the nearly unique concept of an aviator cowboy, Schuyler (Sky) King. Operating from his Flying Crown Ranch near Grover City, Arizona, Sky King (Kirby Grant) would take to the air episode after episode in his Cessna monoplane *Songbird* to break up or track down wrongdoers. Usually his missions were accompanied by teenage niece Penny and/or nephew Clipper. A 1946-50 radio series was followed by TV series that premiered September 16, 1951 and continued until September 1954 under sponsorship of Peter Pan Peanut Butter. The series was picked up again in 1956 for another 10 years under sponsorship of Nabisco.

1

2

3

4

5

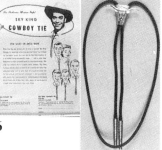

6

7

8

1
SHRINE CIRCUS 14x22″ cardboard poster early 1950s. $100

2
AUTOGRAPHED "KIRBY GRANT" 8x10″ bw photo c. late 1950s. $75

3
SKY KING & PENNY 5.5x7″ full color Nabisco contest postcard c. late 1950s. $75

4
SKY KING & SONGBIRD 3.5x5.5″ color photo Nabisco logo postcard c. 1950s. $35

5
SKY KING 7.5x11.5″ "Navajo Treasure Ring" full color Sunday newspaper ad with offer expiration date June 30, 1950. $25

6
SKY KING 4.5x9.5″ enveloped brown string and silvered brass "Cowboy Tie" mail premium with order coupon sheet from Peter Pan Peanut Butter c. early 1950s. PACKAGED $75, LOOSE $25

7
SKY KING 1x3.25x4.25″ mailing box holding "Aztec Indian Ring" with simulated turquoise stone from Peter Pan Peanut Butter 1950. PACKAGED $300, LOOSE $150

8
SKY KING 1x3.25x4″ mailing box holding "Aztec Emerald Calendar Ring" with simulated emerald stone plus order coupon that expires February 1, 1952. PACKAGED $600, LOOSE $400

Smiley (Frog) Burnette (1911–1967)

The rotund, perpetual comic sidekick to cowboys otherwise seriously going about their business, notably Durango Kid (Charles Starrett) and Gene Autry. A carryover from early radio into western films, Burnette was also an accomplished musician said to be proficient with more than 50 instruments. His jovial support roles were typified by attire of black floppy hat, loose neckerchief, hound's-tooth checkered shirt. His one starring role occured in the 1944 Republic film *Call of the Rockies*, but his support performances frequently rivaled in importance that of the leading star.

1
"FIREBRANDS OF ARIZONA"
11x14″ lobby card for 1944 film.
$50

2
"THE WESTERNER" 9x12″ Vol.
1 #1 issue of fan club newsletter
1940. $30

3
AUTOGRAPHED "FROG"
3.5x5.5″ bw photo c. 1950s. $60

4
"STAR DUST ON THE SAGE"
2.75″ bw Dixie Ice Cream cup lid
1942. $15

5
"MOUNTAIN RHYTHM" 2.25″
sepia Dixie Ice Cream cup lid
1949. $12

6
SMILEY BURNETTE 8x10″ full
color Dixie Ice Cream picture with
back film scenes from "Mexicali
Rose" of 1940. $30

7
SMILEY BURNETTE 8x10″ full
color Dixie Ice Cream picture with
back film scenes from "Back In
The Saddle" of 1941. $25

8
"SMILEY BURNETTE FAN
CLUB" 5x7″ bw photo card pic-
turing him and horse "Black Eyed
Nellie" plus 2.5x3.5″ membership
card c. 1940. EACH $20

9
"SMILEY BURNETTE WEST-
ERN" 7.5x10″ Fawcett Vol. 1 #4
comic book for October 1950. $75

10
SMILEY BURNETTE 9x12″ song
folio c. 1937. $30

11
SMILEY BURNETTE 9x12″ song
folio c. 1940. $30

1

2

3

4

5

6

7

8

9

10

11

Straight Arrow

Radio adventure show of late 1940s through early 1950s with hero Steve Adams, a young cattle rancher who was raised by Commanche Indians. Adams would disappear from his Broken Bow Ranch, as the need for law and order dictated, to don outfit and warpaint of his alter ego Straight Arrow; villains were dealt with by Commanche tactics. The program was sponsored solely by Nabisco during its 1948–51 run on Mutual Network.

1

2

3

4

5

6

7

8

9

10

11

1
STRAIGHT ARROW 10.5x14″ coloring book c. 1950. $30

2
STRAIGHT ARROW 10.5x14″ coloring book c. 1950. $30

3
STRAIGHT ARROW 7.5x9″ packaged jigsaw puzzle from series © 1949. EACH $35

4
STRAIGHT ARROW 2x9.5x19″ boxed Selchow & Righter Co. board game © 1950. $75

5
STRAIGHT ARROW 2.5x3.75″ member card 1951. $50

6
STRAIGHT ARROW 17x17″ bwr bandanna © 1949. $60

7
STRAIGHT ARROW 3.25x7.75″ carded slide ring for bandanna © 1949. CARDED $100, LOOSE $40

8
STRAIGHT ARROW 4x7.5″ "Injun-Uity" box insert card c. 1949-1950. EACH CARD $2

9
STRAIGHT ARROW 4x7.5″ "72 Injun-Uities" bound individual card (see item #8) reprints in two volumes. 1949-1950. $50

10
STRAIGHT ARROW 5.25″ dia. by 12.25″ tall cardboard "War Drum" with wood beater 1949-1950. $200

11
STRAIGHT ARROW 7.5x7.5″ punch-out puppets sheet for Nabisco TV Puppet Theater c. 1952. $25

Sunset Carson (b. 1922)

A tall (6'6") rugged cowboy star from mid-1940s to 1950, very adept from actual experience in cowboy skills of riding, roping, sharpshooting. An international rodeo performer and later a trick rider in the Tom Mix Circus, Carson's acting debut was in the 1943 non-western film *Stage Door Canteen* under his real name of Michael Harrison. His picturesque cowboy name was acquired for his first cowboy role in the 1944 Republic film *Call of the Rockies* in support of leading star Smiley Burnette. Although his heyday acting career consisted of only about 20 films, Carson was one of his era's best-known stars due to live performances in numerous countries around the world.

1
AUTOGRAPHED "SUNSET CARSON" 8x10" bw photo c. late 1940s. $50

2
AUTOGRAPHED "SUNSET CARSON" 8.5x11" tinted photo c. late 1940s. $50

3
AUTOGRAPHED "SUNSET CARSON" 6.5x8.5" sepia photo c. late 1940s. $50

4
SUNSET CARSON 8.5x11" "Sharp Shooting" photo magazine titling him "America's No. 1 Action Cowboy" c. late 1940s. $40

5
AUTOGRAPHED "SUNSET CARSON" 8.5x11" "Sharp Shooting" photo program c. late 1940s. $60

6
"SUNSET CARSON RIDES AGAIN" 11x14" movie lobby card 1948. $20

7
SUNSET CARSON 8x10" school tablet with full color cover photo c. 1950. $20

8
"SUNSET CARSON AND THE BLACK BANDIT" 10.5x12" album holding three 78 rpm records by Action Records, Hollywood c. late 1940s. $30

9
SUNSET CARSON 26" long green felt pennant lettered in white with tinted portrait c. late 1940s. $30

1

2

3

4

5

6

7

8

9

Tales of the Texas Rangers

Late 1950s TV series based on law enforcement activities of the actual Texas Rangers although in no constant time era. Adventure settings varied episode to episode from the mid-1850s to contemporary Texas with crimefighting techniques displayed from that particular period. The series co-starred Willard Parker as Ranger Jace Pearson and Harry Lauter as Ranger Clay Morgan. It aired 1955–1957 on CBS and returned on ABC in 1958–1959.

2

1

3

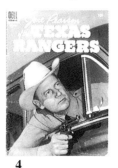

4

5

6

1
JACE PEARSON 5x7″ bw photo with facsimile signature c. late 1950s. $20

2
HARRY LAUTER/WILLARD PARKER 3.25x5.25″ bw exhibit card with facsimile signatures late 1950s. $8

3
''JACE PEARSON'S TALES OF THE TEXAS RANGERS'' 1.5x8.5x16.5″ boxed All-Fair board game © 1956. $30

4
''JACE PEARSON OF THE TEXAS RANGERS'' 7.5x10″ Dell comic book #9 for February-April 1955. $15

5
''TALES OF THE TEXAS RANGERS'' 10.5x14″ Saalfield frame tray inlay jigsaw puzzle c. 1957. $40

6
''TALES OF THE TEXAS RANGERS'' .5x3x4.5″ mailing box holding Curtiss Candy premium of ''Deputy'' membership card, metal star badge, adjustable ring late 1950s. BOX $25, CARD $25, BADGE $50, RING $75

Tales of Wells Fargo

Late 1950s to early 1960s TV series starring Dale Robertson as Jim Hardie, agent for Wells Fargo & Co. Express stageline during the 19th century. Although stage hold-up attempts were an obvious and frequent peril, Hardie was equally confronted by problems of weather, nature, hostile Indians. The series aired March 18, 1957 through September 8, 1962 on NBC, expanding to hour length and increased cast during the final year.

1
TV GUIDE 5x7.5″ issue for July 19, 1958. $15

2
"VERMONT VIDEO GUIDE" 5.5x8″ issue for August 31, 1958. $15

3
DALE ROBERTSON/JIM HARDIE 5x7″ bw photo c. 1960. $12

4
DALE ROBERTSON 3.5x5.5″ color photo postcard picturing "Buick 'Wells Fargo' Built Especially For Dale Robertson" by TV series sponsor c. 1958-1959. $20

5
DALE ROBERTSON/TALES OF WELLS FARGO 3.75x5″ silver/red fabric patch with peel-off backing issued by TV sponsor Buick © 1959. $20

6
"WELLS FARGO AND DANGER STATION" 6x8″ Whitman hardcover book © 1958. $15

7
"TALES OF WELLS FARGO" 8.5x10″ Whitman coloring book © 1957. $30

8
"TALES OF WELLS FARGO COMIC ALBUM" 7x10″ English published book c. 1958. $25

9
"TALES OF WELLS FARGO ANNUAL" 7.25x10″ English published book © 1959. $25

10
"TALES OF WELLS FARGO" 3x11x30.5″ molded stiff cardboard guitar with plastic neck by Rich Toys c. 1960. $85

1

2

3

4

5

6

7

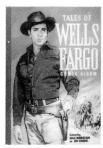

8

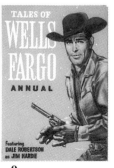

9

10

11

12

13

11
JIM HARDIE 3x8.5x9.5″ boxed full size figure and horse set by Hartland Plastics c. late 1950s. BOXED $250, LOOSE $125

12
JIM HARDIE 8″ tall figure by Hartland Plastics c. late 1950s. BOXED $250, LOOSE $150

13
JIM HARDIE 7x11.5″ carded small size figure and horse by Hartland Plastics © 1960. CARDED $100, LOOSE $60

14

15

14
"WELLS FARGO" 1.5x9.5x19″ boxed Milton Bradley board game © 1959. $45

15
"WELLS FARGO" 1x7x10″ boxed Milton Bradley board game © 1959. $30

16

17

16
"WELLS FARGO" 9.5″ leather holster holding 7″ cap gun in original pack late 1950s. PACKAGED $100, LOOSE $50

17
"WELLS FARGO" 3x10x13″ boxed leather holster set and pair of 10″ cap guns late 1950s. BOXED $275, LOOSE $150

18
"WELLS FARGO" 12x13x4″ tall flocked plastic hat late 1950s. $25

19
"DALE ROBERTSON" child's woven synthetic fabric sweater c. late 1950s. $75

20
"WELLS FARGO" 1x6.5x10″ boxed Milton Bradley jigsaw puzzle © 1959. $30

21
"WELLS FARGO" DALE ROBERTSON 11.5x14.5″ Whitman frame puzzle © 1959. $20

22
"TALES OF WELLS FARGO" 9.25″ dia. white china plate with color art © 1959. $40

18

19

20

21

22

Tex Ritter (1905–1974)

Although probably best remembered as a singing cowboy, Tex Ritter films of his 1936–1945 acting career were second to none in quantity of fistfights, shootouts and general cowboy scrapping. A Texan by birth, Woodward Maurice Ritter began his entertainment career as a ballad singer over a Houston radio station before successfully testing his talent in New York City. His radio early years included a major role on the *Bobby Benson Show* and his film debut was in *Song of the Gringo* released in 1936. He starred in more than 60 films before moving on to many and varied musical interests plus other entertainment areas including an occasional return to films.

1
"HEADIN' FOR THE RIO GRANDE" 27x41" movie poster 1936. $150

2
"RHYTHM OF THE RIO GRANDE" 14x36" movie poster 1940. $30

3
TEX RITTER 5x7" tinted bw photo c. 1940. $20

4
"RIDERS OF SUNDOWN" 2.75" Dixie Ice Cream cup lid c. late 1930s. $20

5
"SUNDOWN ON THE PRAIRIE" 2.25" Dixie Ice Cream cup lid 1939. $15

6
"HIPPODROME" 6.5x9.5" bw announcement for upcoming performance including horse White Flash c. late 1930s. $25

7
TEX RITTER 8x10" Dixie Ice Cream color picture 1938. $20

8
TEX RITTER 8x10" Dixie Ice Cream color picture 1939. $20

9
"ROLLIN' PLAINS" 9x12" sheet music © 1937. $15

10
TEX RITTER 9x12" song folio © 1941. $20

11
TEX RITTER 10.5x12" record album c. late 1940s. $25

12
TEX RITTER 10x10" record album c. late 1940s. $20

1

2

3

4

5

6

7

8

9

10

11

12

Tim Holt (1918–1973)

John Charles Holt, Jr., later to be Tim, had little distance to travel in beginning his Hollywood career. He was born there, the home of his father, Jack Holt, a prominent leading man in the silent film era. Young Tim's film debut at age 10 was in his father's Paramount film *The Vanishing Pioneer* of 1928. His first western major role came in 1938 and before his retirement in 1952, RKO Pictures starred him in more than 50 westerns in a busy annual schedule interrupted by three years of World War II service. Holt flew nearly 60 Pacific Theater combat missions as a bombardier before resuming acting in 1946.

1

3

4

5

6

7

8

9

10

11

1
"THE FARGO KID" 27x41" movie poster of 1940. $150

2
"SIX-GUN GOLD" 27x41" movie poster of 1941. $125

3
"BROTHERS IN THE SADDLE" 27x41" movie poster of 1949. $75

4
"RIDING THE WIND" 11x14" movie lobby card of 1942. $25

5
"RIO GRANDE PATROL" 11x14" movie lobby card of 1950. $15

6
"LAND OF THE OPEN RANGE" 2.75" Dixie Ice Cream cup lid of 1942. $20

7
TIM HOLT 8x10" Dixie Ice Cream color picture of 1942. $25

8
TIM HOLT 8x10" Dixie Ice Cream color picture of 1950. $20

9
TIM HOLT 7.5x10" A-1 comic book #17 for September-October 1948. $80

10
TIM HOLT 1x12x15" boxed lithographed tin two-sided target board with accessories c. 1951. BOXED $75, LOOSE $50

11
TIM HOLT 8x10" school tablet with color photo cover c. 1950. $20

Tim McCoy (1891–1978)

Scholar, historian, war hero, gentleman, cowboy star all befit Col. Tim McCoy whose Colonel rank was earned rapidly during World War I to become a common prefix to his name thereafter. McCoy's entry into western films in 1923 was facilitated by his extensive working knowledge of American Indian oral languages and sign languages. His prolific film career included more than 80 starring roles spanning more than 40 years, interrupted only by an early 1940s volunteered return to military service during World War II. Most of the western life depicted in his films, particularly concerning Indians, was close to authentic rather than the typical glamorized style. His later years continued his lifelong interest in U.S. western history. His live appearances in Wild West shows continued into the early 1970s.

1
"THE OUTLAW DEPUTY"
11x17" movie pressbook 1935.
$50

2
"WEST OF RAINBOW'S END"
27x41" movie poster 1938. $200

3
TIM McCOY 8x10" bw photo
1930s. $40

4
"LIGHTNING BILL CARSON"
2.75" Dixie Ice Cream cup lid of
1936. $20

5
TIM McCOY 8x10" Dixie Ice
Cream color picture mid-1930s.
$40

6
TIM McCOY 8x10" Dixie Ice
Cream color picture of 1936. $30

7
TIM McCOY 8x10" Dixie Ice
Cream picture of 1938. $30

8
TIM McCOY 3.5x4.5" Whitman
Big Little Book c. 1934. $50

9
TIM McCOY 3.5x4.5" Whitman
Big Little Book © 1937. $40

10
TIM McCOY 3.5x4.5" Whitman
Better Little Book © 1939. $35

11
TIM McCOY/DAISY AIR RIFLE
10.25x13.5" ad 1936. $15

12
TIM McCOY 6x8" Wheaties box
back panel c. mid-1930s. $40

1

2

3

4

5

6

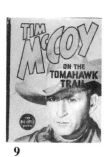

7

8

9

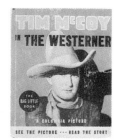

10

11

12

Tom Mix (1880–1940)

Tom Mix was the first cowboy film hero of fast-action, flashy, showmanship style to become a household name. His early life, historically a combination of fact, legend and probably some latter-day press agentry, included valorous army service in Cuba, the Philippines, China, South Africa; law enforcement duties in four states; several national rodeo rider championships.

Historians generally agree that his film career began from employment as foreman and rodeo performer for the Miller Bros. 101 Ranch (apparently named after its 101,000 acres) near Bliss, Oklahoma. There he was spotted and hired away by the (Col. William) Selig Polyscope Movie Co., a very early and primitive maker of documentary style silent shorts. Mix filmed as a western actor for Selig until the company's financial collapse in 1917.

The better known era of his movies began in 1917 under William Fox Productions followed by his move to FBO (Film Booking Office) in 1928, Universal Pictures in 1932–1933, and culminated by his first chapter serial and last film performance in 1935 for Mascot Studios, *The Miracle Rider*. At that time he was 55 years old and hampered by the toll of more than 80 lifetime injuries acquired largely through his insistence on performing movie action stunts personally.

Throughout his film career and concurrent years as live performer for circus shows, his co-star was his trick performing steed, Tony the Wonder Horse, or descendant Tony Jr. The 1924–1932 years began Tom's live performances with Sells Floto Circus. In 1934 he purchased Gill Circus, renamed it Tom Mix Circus, and toured the United States and foreign countries.

Ralston Cereal Co. used Tom's popularity to promote its product for nearly 18 years. Ralston sponsored the Tom Mix radio show, begun in 1933, although there is no record that he ever personally appeared in the show. Nevertheless thousands of youngsters faithfully started the day on Ralston Cereal which, in turn, offered boxtop premiums to the faithful. More than 270 premiums were offered up to the mid-1950 departure of the show from the air. Virtuous qualities, as well as cereal consumption, were expected of Ralston youth assured by Tom's guarantee "Straight Shooters Always Win."

Tom Mix tragically died in 1940 from injury in a car accident. In 1982–1983 Ralston revived the Straight Shooters as a 50th anniversary tribute; a few contemporary premiums were offered but youthful fervor for Tom Mix had long since passed. But to earlier generations of Straight Shooters, the awe, admiration and memory of Tom Mix waver not. The Miracle Rider still rides in the hearts and minds of countless collectors.

1

2

3

4

5

6

1
"THE DAREDEVIL" 27x41″ movie poster of 1920. $800

2
"PRAIRIE TRAILS" 27x41″ movie poster of 1921. $800

3
'THE MIRACLE RIDER' 20x28″ Dutch poster for 1935 movie serial but c. 1940s. $150

4
"A RIDIN' ROMEO" 8.5x11″ English published movie press-book c. 1921. $75

5
"FOR BIG STAKES" 9x12″ English published movie pressbook c. 1922. $75

6
"FLAMING GUNS" 6x9″ movie herald of 1932. $50

7
"THE MIRACLE RIDER"
11x14″ movie lobby cards from
set of eight of 1935. TITLE
CARD $300, SCENE CARD $100

8
"THE MIRACLE RIDER" 3x5″
movie handbill of 1935. $100

9
"HOLLYWOOD DOLLIES"
11x14″ paperdoll sheet featuring
Tom and both non-western and
western outfit © 1925. $175

10
TOM MIX 6.5x10.25″ full color
embossed cigar box label c.
1930s. $75

11
TOM MIX 4.5x5.25″ full color
embossed cigar box label c.
1930s. $75

12
TOM MIX 2.25x3″ full color embossed cigar box label c. 1930s.
$50

13
"JUST TONY" 3.5x5.5″ Oh Boy
Gum card picturing scene from
1922 movie. $15

14
"TOM MIX SAVES THE DAY"
2.5x2.75″ booklet #8 from numbered set of 48 by National Chicle
Gum © 1934. EACH $30

15
TOM MIX 3.25x5.25″ exhibit
card c. 1920s. $12

16
TOM MIX 2x3.25″ card from
"Stars Of The Movie World" set
of 80 by American Caramel Co.
c. 1920s. $15

17
TOM MIX 1.5x2.75″ card #17
from English series of 25 cigarette
cards listing movie titles on back
from 1926-1927. $15

7

8

9

10

11

12

13

14

15

16

17

20

18   **19**

21   **22**

23   **24**

27

25   **26**

28

29

18
TOM MIX 3.5x5.5″ bw photo card c. 1920s. $35

19
TOM MIX 3.5x5.5″ tinted color photo postcard with chest initial logo believed for Selig film company c. 1915. $35

20
TOM MIX 8x10″ Dixie Ice Cream color picture c. mid-1930s. $100

21
''HOME OF TOM MIX'' 3.5x5.5″ color postcard showing residence in Beverly Hills c. 1930s. $15

22
''TOM MIX CIRCUS AND WILD WEST'' 28x42″ paper poster in design of colorful Indian rug c. 1930s. $150

23
''TOM MIX CIRCUS'' 28x49″ color poster for date that documents to 1937. $250

24
''SELLS FLOTO CIRCUS'' 5.75x9″ program from 1929 performances including those by Tom and Tony pictured inside. $90

25
''SELLS FLOTO CIRCUS'' 7x10″ ''Life Of Tom Mix'' souvenir program from 1929. $100

26
''SELLS FLOTO CIRCUS'' 10x16″ newspaper flier © 1930. $100

27
''TOM MIX CIRCUS'' 3.75x5.25″ ticket mid-1930s. $40

28
''TOM MIX CIRCUS AND WILD WEST'' 22″ felt pennant mid-1930s. $125

29
''SELLS FLOTO CIRCUS'' 1.75x3.5″ ticket dated for May 22 performance that documents to 1930. $60

30
TOM MIX 4x5.5″ Fast-Action Story book © 1936. $75

31
TOM MIX 1.5x4.5x6.5″ boxed Whitman Big Little Kit of 384 individual coloring sheets © 1937. $150

32
TOM MIX 1x8x10″ boxed ''Big Little Book Picture Puzzles'' by Whitman © 1938. $75

33
TOM MIX 4.5x5″ Five Star Library book © 1934. $75

34
TOM MIX 4.5x5.5″ Engel-Van Wiseman book © 1934. $75

35
TOM MIX 3.5x4.5″ Whitman Big Little Book © 1935. $100

36
TOM MIX 3.5x4.5″ Whitman Big Little Book based on movie ''Terror Trail'' © 1934. $50

37
TOM MIX 3.5x4.5″ Whitman Big Little Book © 1937. $40

38
TOM MIX 3.5x4.5″ Whitman Big Little Book © 1937. $40

39
TOM MIX 3.5x4.5″ Whitman Better Little Book © 1940. $40

40
''TONY AND HIS PALS'' 7x8″ hardcover book © 1938. $50

41
TOM MIX 11x14″ Whitman coloring book © 1935. $100

42
TOM MIX 6x8″ hardcover book © 1948. $50

43
''TOM MIX RODEO ROPE'' 6x7.25″ folded instruction leaflet for rope spinning by Mordt Co., rope maker, © 1928. $40

44
''TOM MIX WESTERN'' 7.5x10″ Fawcett comic book Vol. 1 #4 for April 1948. $75

30

31

32

33

34

35

36

37

38

39

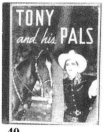

40

41

42

43

44

45

46

47

45
"TOM MIX FOX TROT" 9x12" sheet music c. 1920s. $70

46
"THROWIN' STONES AT THE SUN" 9x12" sheet music picturing Ralston Straight Shooters singing group © 1934. $40

47
"TOM MIX WESTERN SONGS" 9x12" folio © 1935. $40

48

49

48
"TOM MIX CIRCUS GAME" 9x18" closed Parker Brothers game board that opens to 18x18" playing surface c. mid-1930s. $75

49
"TOM MIX CIRCUS GAME" 1x4x5" box of playing pieces for game #48 c. mid-1930s. $50

50

50
"TOM MIX SHOOTING GAL-LERY" 1.5x9.5x12.5" boxed Parker Brothers diecut rigid cardboard target game © 1935. $300

51

51
"WILDCAT" 1x4x5.5" boxed Parker Brothers game of 65 cards and instruction sheet © 1935. $75

52
"TOM MIX RADIO RIFLE" 9x11.5" sales folder for arcade-style target shooting game by Rock-ola c. 1930s. $125

53
"TOM MIX POCKET KNIFE" 6x24" paper store sign by Imperial Knife Co. c. 1930s. $250

52

53

54
TOM MIX 17x17″ bandanna with
art in purple/brown/maroon on
white c. 1930s. $75

55
TOM MIX 8″ long pair of tan
suede leather gloves with inked
portrait on each gauntlet c. 1930s.
$100

56
TOM MIX 8.25x10.5″ "Series
B" set of five bw photos also is-
sued in "A Series" as Ralston
premiums 1933-1934. SET OF
FIVE $100

57
"THE TRAIL OF THE TERRI-
BLE 6" 3x3.5″ Ralston premium
booklet of 1935. $65

58
TOM MIX 12x14″ diecut full
color stiff paper mask Ralston premium of 1934. $250

59
TOM MIX 5x7″ earliest Ralston
premium manual © 1933. $100

60
TOM MIX 5x7″ enlarged and revised second edition of Ralston
manual © 1933. $75

61
TOM MIX 5x7″ Ralston manual
1941. $60

62
TOM MIX 5x7″ Ralston manual
1944. $60

63
TOM MIX 6x9″ Ralston manual
1945, later issued in unauthorized
reproduction (see page 5). $60

64
TOM MIX 5.25x8.5″ first Ralston
premium catalogue of 1933. $50

65
TOM MIX 3x5″ folded Ralston
premium catalogue 1935. $40

66
TOM MIX 3x4″ folded Ralston
premium catalogue sheet 1938.
$40

54

55

56

57

58

59

60

61

62

63

64

65

66

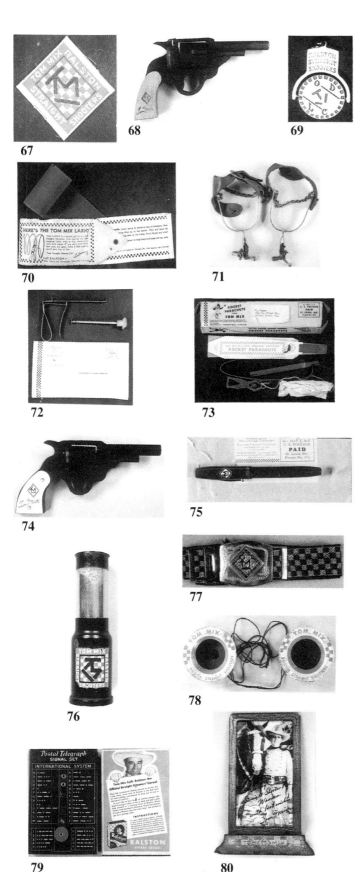

67
TOM MIX 2.5x2.5″ Ralston premium rwb cloth patch 1933. $60

68
TOM MIX 9″ wood gun with stamped grip and barrel that opens with revolving cylinder 1933. $150

69
TOM MIX 1.25x1.5″ Good Luck Spinner 1933. $50

70
TOM MIX 2.5x4″ crepe paper ''Lario'' streamer 1933. $150

71
TOM MIX boot spurs 1933 and later. $200

72
TOM MIX 5.5″ ''Zyp Gun'' in 4.5x8″ mailing envelope 1934. PACKAGED $400, LOOSE $200

73
TOM MIX 1x2x9″ boxed ''Rocket Parachute'' 1936. BOXED $150, LOOSE $100

74
TOM MIX 9″ wood gun with stamped paper grips and barrel that does not break open 1936. $175

75
TOM MIX 5″ fountain pen with 2.5x7″ mailing envelope 1936. ENVELOPE $40, PEN $100

76
TOM MIX 2.5″ telescope of 1937. $75

77
TOM MIX 29″ fabric belt with brass buckle 1936. $150

78
TOM MIX 2″ dia. telephone set joined by string 1938. $75

79
TOM MIX 1x5x7.5″ cardboard ''Postal Telegraph Signal Set'' 1938. $75

80
TOM MIX 2.5x4.75″ tall Ralston premium silvered frame bw photo personalized by first name of recipient 1938. $75

81
TOM MIX 9″ cardboard periscope 1939. $60

82
TOM MIX 1.5x2″ "Gold Ore" watch fob 1940. $60

83
TOM MIX 6.25x9.25″ "Gold Ore Certificate" 1940. $75

84
TOM MIX 1x2.25x4.5″ cardboard "Telegraph Set" 1940. BOXED $125, LOOSE $100

85
TOM MIX 1.5x2″ "Dobie County Sheriff" badge 1946. PACK-AGED $150, BADGE $75

86
TOM MIX glow plastic belt with brass secret compartment buckle 1946. BOXED $200, LOOSE $100

87
TOM MIX 1.25x3x5.25″ boxed aluminum spurs with rowels of lu-minous plastic 1949. BOXED $175, LOOSE $100

88
TOM MIX 4.5x7.25″ photo of Curley Bradley, the radio voice of Tom Mix c. 1946. $75

89
"SELLS FLOTO CIRCUS" 1.75″ button with single shot cap gun and holster c. 1930. $100

90
"TOM MIX CIRCUS" 1.75″ but-ton with "Tom Mix" miniature felt hat c. mid-1930s. $150

91
TOM MIX 9x12″ enveloped Ral-ston 50th anniversary kit 1982-1983. CARD $10, PATCH $20, COMIC $15

92
TOM MIX 1.25″ Ralston 50th an-niversary watch 1982-1983. $250

93
TOM MIX 2.5″ tall by 5.5″ dia. Ralston 50th anniversary ceramic cereal bowl 1982-1983. $25

81

82

83

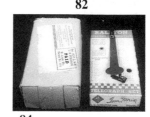

84

85

86

87

88   **89**   **90**

91   **92**   **93**

Wagon Train

A sprawling TV series that vividly related the innumerable perils and problems besetting a pioneer covered-wagon caravan enroute from Missouri to California. Original co-stars were Ward Bond as Wagonmaster Seth Adams and Robert Horton as Trail Scout Flint McCullough. Following Bond's death late in 1960, John McIntire succeeded as Wagonmaster Chris Hale. The series, featuring a weekly top-name guest star as the subject of that episode's adventure, was TV's highest-rated western in its 1961–1962 season. The *Wagon Train* title was used previously as a 1940 Tim Holt movie, and Ward Bond was featured in a similar 1950 *Wagonmaster* film directed by John Ford.

1
TV GUIDE 5x7.5″ issue for April 11, 1959. $20

2
TV GUIDE 5x7.5″ issue for November 19, 1960. $15

3
TV GUIDE 5x7.5″ issue for December 7, 1963. $15

4
''VERMONT VIDEO GUIDE'' 5.25x8.25″ issue for August 2, 1959. $20

5
''MAJOR ADAMS'' 13x16″ cardboard poster for ABC-TV Sunday afternoon reruns 1963-64. $100

6
HORTON & BOND 8x10″ bw photo c. 1958. $25

7
WAGON TRAIN 2.5x3.5″ gum card from series of six in 71-card ''T.V. Westerns'' set by Topps Gum © 1958. EACH $5

8
WAGON TRAIN 8.5x11″ Whitman coloring book © 1959. $40

9
WAGON TRAIN 6x8″ Whitman hardcover book © 1959. $35

10
''WAGON TRAIN ANNUAL'' 8.5x11.5″ English hardcover book © 1959. $30

11
''WAGON TRAIN ANNUAL'' 8.5x11.5″ English hardcover book © 1961. $25

12
''WAGON TRAIN ANNUAL'' 7x10″ English hardcover book © 1962. $25

13
SETH ADAMS 3x8.5x9.5″ boxed
large size figure and horse by
Hartland Plastics c. late 1950s.
BOXED $250, LOOSE $150

14
WAGON TRAIN 2x9x14.5″ boxed
leather belt and double holster set
holding silvered metal cap guns
with white plastic grips. By Leslie-Henry Co. © 1958. BOXED
$350, LOOSE $200

15
WAGON TRAIN 3x12x27″ boxed
''Cowboy Outfit'' of plastic rifle,
metal spurs, leather holster hold-
ing metal and plastic cap gun. By
Leslie-Henry Co. c. 1958.
BOXED $300, LOOSE $200

16
WAGON TRAIN 4x13x24″ boxed
Marx Toys playset late 1950s.
$800

17
WAGON TRAIN 5x15x21″ boxed
Marx Toys playset late 1950s.
$500

18
WAGON TRAIN 2x7.5x10.5″
boxed English battery operated
projector plus films by Bell Toy
Production, London © 1960. $100

19
WAGON TRAIN 7.25x9.5x23.5″
boxed plastic and fabric replica
wagon with figures and horses by
Marx Toys c. 1960. BOXED
$150, LOOSE $100

20
''WAGON TRAIN/MAJOR AD-
AMS'' 7x9″ leather saddle for
rocking horse or bicycle seat with
7″ long flank strips suspended
from each side c. 1960. $75

21
WAGON TRAIN 11.5x14.5″
Whitman frame tray inlay jigsaw
puzzle c. late 1950s. $20

22
WAGON TRAIN 4x7x8.5″ flat
steel lunch box by King-Seeley
Co. © 1964. BOX $125, BOT-
TLE (NOT SHOWN) $50

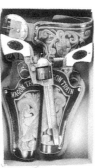

13　　**14**

15

16　　**17**

18

19

20　　　**21**　　　**22**

Wanted—Dead or Alive

Absorbing TV series starring Steve McQueen as the brooding, intense bounty hunter Josh Randall, who expedited his hunts and capture of criminals by a trusty sawed-off Winchester carbine rifle affectionately titled ''Mare's Laig.'' The series launched the brief but phenomenally successful screen career of McQueen prior to his untimely death in 1980. The show premiered September 6, 1958 and continued through 94 episodes before leaving the air March 29, 1961.

1

2

3

4

5

6

7

8

9

10

1
''WANTED: DEAD OR ALIVE'' 2.5x3.5″ card from series of five in 71-card ''T.V. Western'' set by Topps Gum © 1958. EACH $5

2
SIGNED ''STEVE McQUEEN'' 4x5″ photo c. 1960. $150

3
JOSH RANDALL 3x8.5x9.5″ boxed large size figure and horse by Hartland Plastics c. late 1950s. BOXED $350, LOOSE $200

4
WANTED-DEAD OR ALIVE 2x9x17.5″ boxed Lowell Toy board game c. late 1950s. $125

5
''THE PURSUER'' 3x8.5x17″ boxed unauthorized plastic sawed-off rifle and accessories late 1950s. BOXED $150, LOOSE $75

6
''MARE'S LAIG'' 1x16x16″ boxed target and dart rifle © 1959. BOXED $250, LOOSE $150

7
''MARE'S LAIG'' 7x15″ carded 13.5″ cap gun c. 1959. CARDED $250, LOOSE $125

8
''MARE'S LAIG'' 2x12x20″ boxed 19″ gun plus accessories c. 1959. BOXED $300, LOOSE $150

9
''MARE'S LAIG'' 8.5x15″ carded gun with holster c. 1959. CARDED $200, LOOSE $125

10
''MARE'S LAIG'' 4x7.5″ carded cap gun c. 1959. CARDED $75, LOOSE $35

Wild Bill Hickok

One of TV's earliest western series based loosely on the actual gunfighter marshal of the 19th century and several movie versions including those starring William S. Hart, Bill Elliott, Roy Rogers. The TV version starred handsome matinee idol Guy Madison in the title role closely supported by gravel-voiced Andy Devine as fumbling sidekick Jingles. The TV series ran through 113 episodes between 1951 and 1958 in original run; a radio series, also starring Madison and Devine, ran concurrently throughout 1956.

1
"THE TITLED TENDERFOOT" 27x41″ movie poster 1955. $100

2
"BEHIND SOUTHERN LINES" 11x14″ movie lobby card of 1952. $25

3
GUY MADISON 3.5x5.25″ bw photo fan postcard c. 1954. $20

4
ANDY DEVINE 3.5x5.5″ color photo exhibit card c. 1950s. $8

5
HICKOK & JINGLES 11x14″ Saalfield coloring book © 1953. $40

6
HICKOK & JINGLES 8.5x11″ Saalfield coloring book © 1957. $35

7
WILD BILL HICKOK 6.5x8″ Rand McNally Elf book © 1956. $15

8
WILD BILL HICKOK 6.5x8″ Rand McNally Elf book © 1956. $15

9
"SIX-GUN HEROES" 7.5x10″ Charlton comic book Vol. 4 #41 for May 1957. $15

10
HICKOK "CAVALRY AND THE INDIANS" 1.5x7.5x14″ boxed Built-Rite board game c. mid-1950s. $50

11
HICKOK & JINGLES "PONY EXPRESS" 1.5x7.5x14″ boxed Built-Rite board game © 1956. $40

1

2

3

4

5

6

7

8

9

10

11

12

13

12
HICKOK & JINGLES 2.5x11x14″ boxed gun and holster set mid-1950s. BOXED $350, LOOSE $175

13
HICKOK & JINGLES 2x11.5x11.5″ boxed gun and holster set © 1955. BOXED $250, LOOSE $125

14

15

16

14
HICKOK 2x6.5x8″ boxed Built-Rite jigsaw puzzle © 1956. $20

15
WILD BILL HICKOK 11x13.5″ Built-Rite frame tray inlay jigsaw puzzle c. mid-1950s. $25

16
WILD BILL HICKOK 4x5.5″ set of Tru-Vue stereo cards c. mid-1950s. $35

17

18

19

17
HICKOK 1.5x6x7.25″ Sugar Corn Pops box c. 1952. $125

18
JINGLES 2x7.5x9.5″ Sugar Pops box early 1950s. $125

19
JINGLES 2x7.5x9.5″ Sugar Corn Pops box early 1950s. $125

20
HICKOK & JINGLES 6½′ base dia. by 5′ tall child's canvas "Indian Country" tent with poles and accessories c. mid-1950s. $125

21
WILD BILL & JINGLES 5″ tall plastic tumbler milk company premium c. mid-1950s. $60

21

22
HICKOK & JINGLES 4x7x8″ flat steel lunch box and 6.5″ steel bottle with plastic cup set by Aladdin Industries © 1955. BOX $125, BOTTLE $60

23
HICKOK & JINGLES 4x6″ carded metal star badge © 1955. CARDED $75, LOOSE $50

20

22

23

The Wild, Wild West

Unique western TV series featuring fantasy, bizarre, whimsical and humorously absurd adventures caused by equally fanciful assorted villains and culprits. Co-starred were Robert Conrad as James West and Ross Martin as Artemus Gordon, both special agents appointed by President U.S. Grant to ferret out and vanquish ne'er-do-wells throughout the west. The pair traveled through their frontier adventures in a railroad car stocked by a zany arsenal of equipment and devices to foil each creative antagonist. The series premiered September 17, 1965 and continued in original run through September 19, 1969.

1
TV TIMES 5.5x8.5″ issue for January 9, 1966. $25

2
TV GUIDE 5x7.5″ issue for January 6, 1968. $25

3
"THE WILD WILD WEST" 4.25x7″ Signet Books first printing paperback 1966. $25

4
AUTOGRAPHED "ROSS MARTIN" AND "ROBERT CONRAD" 11x14″ matted display of bw photo above individual signatures c. late 1960s. $150

5
"THE WILD, WILD WEST" 7.5x10″ Gold Key comic book #3 from 1968. $20

6
"THE WILD, WILD WEST" 7.5x10″ Gold Key comic book #5 from 1969. $20

7
"THE WILD WILD WEST" 3.5x7x8″ flat steel lunch box by Aladdin Industries © 1969. $150

8
"THE WILD WILD WEST" 7″ tall plastic thermos bottle (from lunch box #7) by Aladdin Industries © 1969. $75

9
"ROSS MARTIN" 8x10″ school tablet with color cover photo c. late 1960s. $40

1

2

3

4

5

6

7

8

9

William S. Hart (1870–1946)

One of the very earliest big name western stars who came to movies following a distinguished theatre career that included Shakespearean roles. A scholar of western lore and American Indians, he began his film career as advisor as well as actor in 1914. In a comparatively brief career ending in 1925, he still appeared in more than 40 westerns. His final film, *Tumbleweeds,* was produced under his direction. He returned to the screen in 1939 to introduce the reissue of this film (his first talking role) but his legacy is from the silent era and his persistence in depicting western adventure in accurate realism rather than contrived action. Hart roles were often of a ''good badman'' rather than pure ''goodman.''

1

2

3

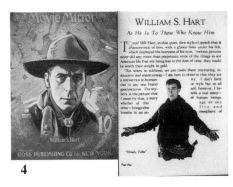

4

5

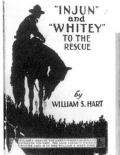

6

7

8

1
WILLIAM S. HART 2x3.25″ bw card from ''Stars Of The Movie World'' 80-card set by American Caramel Co. c. 1920s. $15

2
WILLIAM S. HART 3.25x5.25″ bw exhibit card inscribed for movie ''Three Word Brand'' 1921. $12

3
''WM. HART'' 3.5x5.5″ tinted bw photo exhibit card inscribed for movie ''Two Gun Man'' early 1920s. $12

4
''LITTLE MOVIE MIRROR'' 4.5x6″ biography booklet from movie star series © 1920. $60

5
WILLIAM S. HART 3.5x5.5″ bw English postcard c. 1920s. $20

6
''INJUN AND WHITEY TO THE RESCUE'' 5.5x7.75″ book authored by Hart from ''Golden West Boys'' series by him © 1922. $35

7
''ARKONA'' 10x12″ Australian sheet music for song from Hart film ''White Oak'' of 1921 with 1922 copyright. $50

8
''WM. S. HART'' 1x3x3″ boxed 8mm film ''The New Boss'' for Keystone toy projectors 1930s. $25

Zorro

A most enduring fictional character created originally in 1919 as the hero of strip cartoon by Johnston McCulley. The character of the black-garbed and masked Zorro (Spanish for fox) has been portrayed more than 15 times in film versions beginning in the 1920s and continuing into the 1970s although the Disney TV series of 1957–1959 and subsequent 1960 Disney film *Zorro The Avenger* (all starring Guy Williams) by far prompted the most Zorro collectibles. Other versions before and since include *The Mark of Zorro* (1920) and *Don Q, Son of Zorro* (1925), both silents starring Douglas Fairbanks, Sr.; *The Bold Caballero* (1936) starring Robert Livingston in Republic Pictures' first attempt at color filming; *Zorro Rides Again* (1937) serial starring John Carroll, reissued as a feature film under same title in 1959; *Zorro's Fighting Legion* (1939) serial starring Reed Hadley; *Mark of Zorro* (1940) starring Tyrone Power; *Zorro's Black Whip* (1944) serial starring actress Linda Stirling as the mysterious Black Whip; *The Ghost of Zorro* (1949) serial starring Clayton Moore, reissued as a feature film under same title in 1959. Following the Disney years, other Zorro movie titles and starring characters are *The Sign of Zorro* (1962), Sean Flynn; *Shadow of Zorro* (1962), Frank Latimore; *Zorro vs. Maciste* (1963), Pierre Brice; *Zorro at the Court of Spain* (1963), George Ardisson; *Zorro and the Three Musketeers* (1963), Gordon Scott; *Zorro* (1975), Alain Delon. Most of the latter six are Italian or Italian-Spanish versions. A TV spoof version, *Zorro and Son,* starring Henry Darrow and Paul Regina, began April 6, 1983 and concluded after only nine episodes less than two months later. The original 1920s Zorro is credited by some historians as the inspiration for creation in the early 1930s of another masked hero, The Lone Ranger.

1
TV GUIDE 5x7.5″ issue for April 26, 1958. $50

2
"JUNIOR TV" 5x7.5″ issue for September 1958. $35

3
ZORRO 5x7″ Disney Studios bw photo fan card c. 1960. $30

4
WALT DISNEY'S MAGAZINE 8x11.5″ issue for April 1958. $30

5
ZORRO 9x11″ Big Golden Book © 1958. $30

6
ZORRO 9.5x12.5″ Golden Book © 1958. $20

7
ZORRO 5.5x8″ Whitman hard-cover book © 1958. $15

8
ZORRO 6.75x8″ Little Golden Book © 1958. $12

9
ZORRO 6.75x8″ Little Golden Book © 1958. $12

1

2

3

4

5

6

7

8

9

10

11

12

13

14

15

16

17

18

19

20

21

10
ZORRO 7.5x10″ Gold Key comic book #4 for November 1966. $18

11
ZORRO 12x12″ album of 33 1/3 rpm record featuring Guy Williams © 1958. $25

12
ZORRO 2x3x7″ tall painted china figurine c. 1958. $125

13
ZORRO 2x7x13″ boxed assembly parts for Zorro and horse by Aurora Plastics c. late 1950s. $150

14
ZORRO 10″ tall hand puppet with vinyl head and fabric outfit by Gund Products c. 1958. $75

15
ZORRO 10″ tall hand puppet with vinyl head and hat plus fabric outfit by Gund Products c. late 1950s. $60

16
ZORRO 2″ tall black plastic figure and 2.5″ tall matching plastic horse c. late 1950s. $35

17
ZORRO & HORSE 5″ tall mounted figure set of black rubber with paint accents from Bully of West Germany © 1985. $35

18
ZORRO 2x13x25″ boxed weapons and accessories set by Daisy Mfg. Co. c. 1960. BOXED $400, LOOSE $200

19
ZORRO 6x12x28″ boxed set of weapons, hat and mask by Marx Toys c. late 1950s. BOXED $400, LOOSE $200

20
ZORRO 9x45″ carded plastic and metal "Flintlock Rifle" by Marx Toys c. late 1950s. CARDED $200, LOOSE $100

21
ZORRO 1x4.5x7.5″ boxed Dominoes set by Halsam c. late 1950s. $75

22
ZORRO 7x24″ carded equipment pieces late 1950s. CARDED $150, LOOSE $75

23
ZORRO 2.5x15x20″ boxed Spring Action Target set late 1950s. BOXED $150, LOOSE $75

24
ZORRO 5x5x28″ boxed Fencing Set of two swords, masks and face guards c. late 1950s. BOXED $150, LOOSE $75

25
ZORRO 2x9x10″ boxed cork-shooting gun and four plastic soldier targets c. late 1950s. BOXED $125, LOOSE $75

26
ZORRO 1.5x16x24″ boxed tin target and plastic rifle plus darts c. 1960. BOXED $150, LOOSE $75

27
ZORRO 2x9x17″ boxed Parker Brothers board game © 1966. $50

28
ZORRO 2x7x10″ boxed Jaymar jigsaw puzzle from series of three or more c. 1960. EACH $35

29
ZORRO 12x12x4″ black straw hat with fabric crown label plus black felt face mask c. late 1950s. $50

30
ZORRO 3.5x4.5″ vinyl billfold c. 1960. $40

31
ZORRO 2x5x5″ boxed wristwatch by US Time displayed on replica hat c. late 1950s. BOXED $175, LOOSE $50

32
ZORRO 8x10″ school tablet with reward poster cover design c. 1960. $50

33
ZORRO 2x14x18″ boxed Paint By Numbers set c. 1960. $85

34
ZORRO 1x10x13″ boxed Pencil Color set c. 1960. $85

22

23

24

25

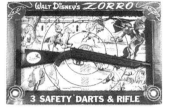

26

27

28

29

30   **31**

32   **33**   **34**

35 **36**

37

38 **39** **40**

41

42

43 **44** **45**

35
ZORRO 4x7x12″ wide vinyl zippered travel bag c. 1960. $60

36
ZORRO 4.5x4.5″ pack of three View-Master stereo reels © 1958. $35

37
ZORRO .5x1x3″ plastic keychain flashlight designed to raise the hat and mask to reveal Zorro's face when lighted. Late 1950s. $50

38
ZORRO 3x7x10.5″ candy box c. late 1950s. $100

39
ZORRO 2.5x3.5″ enveloped "Sun Pictures" kit c. 1960. $25

40
ZORRO 2x6x4.5″ tall figural plastic boot mug with Z-shaped handle c. 1960. $50

41
ZORRO 4x7x8″ flat steel 'Black Sky' version lunch box and 6.5″ steel bottle by Aladdin Industries © 1958. BOX $125, BOTTLE $75

42
ZORRO 4x7x8″ flat steel 'Red Sky' version lunch box and 6.5″ steel thermos by Aladdin Industries © 1966. BOX $150, BOTTLE $100

43
ZORRO 2.25″ brass stickpin topped by 1″ plastic portrait, European made © 1964. $35

44
ZORRO 3.5″ bw pin-back button c. late 1950s. $30

45
ZORRO 3.5″ bw pin-back button with typography variation to #44 c. late 1950s. $30

APPENDIX

WESTERN HISTORY AND ENTERTAINMENT LANDMARKS
A Chronology of Selected Events

1690 The General Court of Massachussetts defines "frontier" limits within the state to maintain a garrison of 40 soldiers at each frontier town.

1732 A stagecoach line is established in New Jersey between Burlington and Amboy with further connections by boat to New York City and Philadelphia. The stage line is the first regular service of its kind in the colonies.

1735 Daniel Boone is born near Reading, Pa.

1765 Conclusion of French-Indian Wars opens vast new tracts for westward expansion.

1775 Daniel Boone with company of 30 men blazes Wilderness Road from Fort Chiswell, Virginia, through Cumberland Gap to Ohio River to found Boonesborough, Kentucky.

1786 Davy Crockett is born in Hawkins County, Tennessee.

1815 The Conestoga Wagon, in limited eastern use since the 1760s, becomes the most efficient mode of transportation for long treks westward. The typical Conestoga required six horses or oxen and was capable of carrying eight tons of cargo. A smaller version is known as The Prairie Schooner.

1820 Daniel Boone dies at 85 years of age in St. Charles, Missouri.

1831 A New York City stage play, *The Lion of the West*, features a frontiersman named Col. Nimrod Wildfire, "a raw Kentuckian recently elected to Congress" in satire of Davy Crockett, then approaching the end of his second term in Congress.

1833 Samuel Colt invents a six-shooter revolver patented February 25. The revolver is the first firearm for convenient use by man on horseback. Colt revolvers rapidly become common.

1836 The Battle of the Alamo in San Antonio, Texas, begins February 23 and ends March 6 against the army of General Santa Anna. Among the U.S. casualties of the massacre are Davy Crockett and Jim Bowie. In April, the Mexican army is defeated under U.S. leadership of Sam Houston.

1841 The first covered wagon train to California departs Sapling Grove, Kansas and arrives near Sonora in early November.

1848 Gold is discovered January 7 at John A. Sutter's mill on the American River near Sacramento, California, to begin the nation's first great westward gold rush.

1850 Beginning July 1, overland mail delivery west of the Missouri River is organized on a monthly basis from Independence, Missouri to Salt Lake City, Utah. Early cattle trails are established.

1852 Two officers of American Express Co., Henry Wells and William G. Fargo, form their new company to provide horseback and stagecoach express delivery service from eastern points to California.

1858 West and east coasts are connected by overland mail service. Delivery from San Francisco to St. Louis was by stage before transfer to train for the rest of eastward journey.

1859   The nation's richest known silver deposit, The Comstock Lode, is discovered in western Nevada.

1860   April 3 begins first relay of Pony Express mail service from Missouri to California. Arrival in Sacramento is April 13. Initial mailing cost was $5 for first half-ounce. Pony Express service was discontinued the following year.

1861   Transcontinental telegraph service is begun. The first use was telegraph message from Sacramento to President Lincoln in Washington, D.C.

1865   The first train robbery of record occurs May 5 at dawn near North Bend, Ohio. An Ohio & Mississippi train is derailed and robbed by looters.

1869   Transcontinental railroad is reality, completed May 10 at Promontory Point, Utah, linking Central Pacific Railroad from the west and Union Pacific Railroad from the east.

1870   Cattles drives begin to flourish, giving rise to the title of cowboy. Common destinations included Abilene, Kansas City, Chicago and other midwestern cities during the next two decades.

1876   General George Custer and troops are massacred June 25 in attack on Sioux Indians and Chief Sitting Bull at Little Bighorn River, Montana.

1878   Wild West Shows originate. Among the earliest showmen is Dr. W. F. Carver, a trick shooter from back of a racing horse.

1883   William F. Cody's ''Buffalo Bill's Wild West Show'' is believed to first perform July 4 in North Platte, Nebraska. The show toured the United States for about 30 years as well as European visits. Among the major performers are Chief Sitting Bull and Annie Oakley.

1885   Fencing of public lands in the west is prohibited by Act of Congress. Fencing disputes continue on private lands.

1887   Teddy Roosevelt calls for formation of ''Boone and Crockett'' Club for protection of game and wildlife.

1889   A pistol shot at noon April 22 opens the great Oklahoma land rush for thousands of settlers to nearly two million acres purchased from Cree and Seminole Indian tribes. The Oklahoma Territory is officially designated in 1890.

1897   The first Frontier Day celebration is held in Cheyenne, Wyoming.

1898   A primitive three-minute still sequence film, *Cripple Creek Bar-Room*, is an attempt to show western saloon life at the turn of the century.

1902   Owen Wister's novel about 1880s Wyoming life, *The Virginian*, is first published. The novel was reprinted 14 times in the next eight months to become one of the most widely read western novels of all time.

1903   *The Great Train Robbery*, a landmark film, is released. Considered to be the first motion picture (and certainly the first western) with a plot, the movie ran nine minutes in length and introduced the first cowboy star in actor Max Aaronson, also known as Max Anderson, G. M. Anderson, and most commonly, Bronco Billy.

1905   Nickleodeon theaters appear. Among the first is one opened in Pittsburgh, Pennsylvania by John P. Harris and Harry Davis. Within the next three years an estimated 10,000 nickleodeons flourish in the United States, drawing an estimated 200,000 customers daily.

1910 Hassan Corktip Cigarettes issues a 50-card insert premium set titled ''Cowboy Series'' picturing and describing true cowboy activities.

1912 Zane Grey novels begin popularity with publication of *Riders of the Purple Sage* followed by more than 50 others by Grey, a New York dentist.

1914 William S. Hart appears in his first western film, *The Bargain*, to begin his 11-year career in silents.

1926 William Boyd makes his western role debut in *The Last Frontier*.

1928 *The Big Hop*, an aviation western starring Buck Jones, is generally considered to be the first western using sound in any form, although in dubbed style. Released later in the year is a legitimate sound film, *Land of the Silver Fox*, starring Rin-Tin-Tin.

1929 The portrayal of Cisco Kid by Warner Baxter in film *In Old Arizona* earns him the first Academy Award for western role actor.

1930 The silent era of western films fades further with release of epic sound feature film, *The Big Trail*, directed by Raoul Walsh and starring an unknown John Wayne. Universal and Mascot Studios also release first of sound chapter serials.

1931 *Cimarron* wins Oscar for best western picture.

1932 *Bobby Benson Adventures* begins on CBS Radio.

1933 *The Lone Ranger* radio series debuts January 30 over WXYZ, Detroit. Ralston Cereal begins sponsorship of *Tom Mix Straight Shooters* radio series. An estimated 530 western films are issued in the 1933–1937 era.

1935 Mascot, Monogram, and Liberty Pictures are merged into new Republic Studios. Tom Mix makes his final film appearance; Gene Autry, Roy Rogers (as Leonard Slye) and William Boyd as Hopalong Cassidy make their western film debuts.

1936 *The Trail of the Lonesome Pine* is the first outdoor film to be shot in three-color ''Technicolor'' process. Paramount Studios is the innovator.

1937 Buck Jones begins brief *Hoofbeats* radio show.

1938 *Red Ryder* debuts as a comic strip character by creator Fred Harman on Sunday, May 6. An estimated 700 western films are issued in the 1938–1941 era.

1940 The *Gene Autry Melody Ranch* radio show begins on CBS sponsored by Wrigley's Gum. Tom Mix is killed in an October 12 car accident.

1942 Buck Jones dies from injuries and burns sustained in Boston's Coconut Grove nightclub fire. An estimated 500 or more western movies or serials are issued in the 1942–1946 era.

1943 Roy Rogers begins 12-year consecutive run as leading money-making western star.

1944 Roy Rogers and Dale Evans first appear together in film *Cowboy and the Senorita*. Sunset Carson debuts as western actor.

1948 Classic western film *The Treasure of Sierra Madre* wins Oscar for director John Huston in addition to Oscars for Best Picture and acting performance of son Walter Huston.

1949 Television introduces two established cowboy heroes. Hopalong Cassidy debuts June 24, The Lone Ranger debuts September 15.

1950   TV debuts three more western series featuring Gene Autry, Gabby Hayes, and Cisco Kid. Rex Allen debuts as a western movie actor.

1951   TV debuts shows of Roy Rogers, Wild Bill Hickok, and Sky King.

1952   Movie *High Noon* wins Oscar for Gary Cooper as actor and Oscar for Best Song for title song sung by Tex Ritter.

1953   TV debuts Annie Oakley series starring Gail Davis, first TV western series based on female lead role.

1954   TV version of Rin-Tin-Tin debuts. First episode of Davy Crockett appears in Disneyland series.

1955   Davy Crockett popularity peaks. Among the major TV series premieres are *Gunsmoke*, *Cheyenne*, *The Life and Legend of Wyatt Earp*. Republic Pictures cease production of western movie serials.

1957   TV western popularity flourishes as 14 new shows begin; only two shows are dropped from preceding season.

1958   Popularity of new TV western shows peaks as 17 new shows are offered with only two cancelled shows from preceding season. A total of 31 westerns were offered in prime time.

1959   Popularity of new TV western shows begins its decline although 15 new shows are offered.

1963   Movie version of *How The West Was Won*, the first feature film to use Cinerama process, wins three Oscars and is nominated for two others.

1964   TV version of Daniel Boone debuts.

1965   Lee Marvin wins Oscar for title role in western movie *Cat Ballou*.

1967   The last year of significant number of new TV western series as six debut during the season.

1969   John Wayne wins acting Oscar for role of Rooster Cogburn in movie *True Grit*.

1978   TV's only new western series is *How The West Was Won*.

1979   John Wayne dies at 72 years of age, three years after his final film, *The Shootist*.

1981   Wrather Productions resurrects the masked man in movie version *The Legend of The Lone Ranger*. Another yesteryear masked hero is resurrected in comic film *Zorro, The Gay Blade*.

1982   Ralston Cereal Co. briefly revives its *Tom Mix Straight Shooters Club* to commemorate the 50th anniversary of original sponsorship on radio.

1988   A TV western series, *Paradise*, debuts as the only such series on major networks. The series is best recalled for guest performances by TV western stars of the 1950s and 1960s.

1993   Resurgence of public and media interest in the western genre. Television movies and series included *The Adventures of Brisco County Jr.*, *Return to Lonesome Dove*, and *Bonanza: The Return*.

1994   Movie comedy version of *Maverick* is released starring Mel Gibson in the title role with James Garner of the late 1950s TV series in supporting cast.

TELEVISION WESTERN SERIES

Listed alphabetically with dates indicating original viewing runs and original network. Later reruns, later syndication, or later network changes are not included.

A

Adventures of Champion, 9/30/55–2/3/56, CBS
Adventures of Jim Bowie, 9/7/56–8/29/58, ABC
Adventures of Kit Carson, 1951–1955, Syndicated
Adventures of Rin-Tin-Tin, 10/15/54–8/28/59, ABC
Adventures of Wild Bill Hickok, 1951–1958, Syndicated
Alaskans, The, 10/4/59–9/25/60, ABC
Alias Smith and Jones, 1/20/71–1/13/73, ABC
Annie Oakley, 1953–1956, Syndicated

B

Bat Masterson, 10/8/59–9/21/61, NBC
Bearcats!, 9/16/71–12/30/71, CBS
Big Valley, The, 9/15/65–5/19/69, ABC
Black Saddle, 1/10/59–9/30/60, NBC
Bonanza, 9/12/59–1/16/73, NBC
Boots and Saddles, 1957–1959, Syndicated
Branded, 1/24/65–9/4/66, NBC
Brave Eagle, 9/28/55–6/6/56, CBS
Bret Maverick, 12/1/81–8/24/82, NBC
Broken Arrow, 9/25/56–9/18/60, ABC
Bronco, 10/20/59–9/13/60, ABC
Buckskin, 7/3/58–9/14/59, NBC
Buffalo Bill Jr., 1955, Syndicated

C

Cade's Country, 9/19/71–9/4/72, CBS
Californians, The, 9/24/57–8/27/59, NBC
Casey Jones, 1958, Syndicated
Champion (see Adventures of)
Cheyenne, 9/20/55–9/13/63, ABC
Cimarron City, 10/11/58–9/16/60, NBC
Cimarron Strip, 9/7/67–9/7/71, CBS
Cisco Kid, The, 1950–1956, Syndicated
Colt .45, 10/18/57–9/27/60, ABC
Cowboy G-Men, 1952, Syndicated
Cowboy in Africa, 9/11/67–9/16/68, ABC
Cowboys, The, 2/6/74–8/14/74, ABC
Crash Corrigan's Ranch, 7/15/50–9/29/50, ABC

D

Dakotas, The, 1/7/63–9/9/63, ABC
Daniel Boone, 9/24/64–8/27/70, NBC
Davy Crockett, 12/15/54–2/23/55, (Disney), ABC
Death Valley Days, 1952–1975, Syndicated
Deputy, The, 9/12/59–9/16/61, NBC

Destry, 2/14/64–9/11/64, ABC
Dick Powell's Zane Grey Theatre, 10/5/56–9/20/62, CBS
Dundee and The Culhane, 9/6/67–12/13/67, CBS

E

Elfego Baca (see Nine Lives of)
Empire, 9/25/62–9/6/64, CBS

F

F Troop, 9/14/65–8/31/67, ABC
Frontier, 9/25/55–9/9/56, NBC
Frontier Circus, 10/5/61–9/20/62, CBS
Frontier Doctor, 1957–1958, Syndicated
Frontier Justice, 7/7/58–9/28/61, CBS
Fury, 9/15/55–9/3/66, NBC

G

Gabby Hayes Show, The, 10/1/50–7/14/56, NBC
Gene Autry Show, 7/23/50–8/7/56, CBS
Grizzly Adams (see Life and Times of)
Guns of Will Sonnett, The, 9/8/67–9/15/69, ABC
Gunslinger, The, 2/9/61–9/14/61, CBS
Gunsmoke, 9/10/55–9/1/75, CBS

H

Have Gun Will Travel, 9/14/57–9/21/63, CBS
Hawkeye (and the Last of the Mohicans), 1957, Syndicated
Hec Ramsey, 10/8/72–8/25/74, NBC
High Chaparral, The, 9/10/67–9/10/71, NBC
Hondo, 9/8/67–12/29/67, ABC
Hopalong Cassidy, 6/24/49–12/23/51, NBC
Hotel De Paree, 10/2/59–9/23/60, CBS
How The West Was Won, 2/12/78–4/23/79, ABC

I

Iron Horse, 9/12/66–1/6/68, ABC

J

Jefferson Drum, 4/25/58–4/23/59, NBC
Jesse James (see Legend of)
Jim Bowie (see Adventures of)
Johnny Ringo, 10/1/58–9/29/60, CBS

K

Kit Carson (see Adventures of)
Klondike, 10/10/60–2/6/61, NBC
Kodiak, 9/13/74–10/11/74, ABC
Kung Fu, 10/14/72–6/28/75, ABC

L

Lancer, 9/24/68–9/9/71, CBS
Laramie, 9/15/59–9/17/63, NBC

Lash of the West, 1/4/53–4/26/53, ABC
Law of the Plainsman, 10/1/59–9/24/62, NBC
Lawman, 10/5/58–10/2/62, ABC
Legend of Jesse James, The, 9/13/65–9/5/66, ABC
Life and Legend of Wyatt Earp, 9/6/55–9/26/61, ABC
Life and Times of Grizzly Adams, 2/9/77–7/26/78, NBC
Little House on the Prairie, 9/11/74–3/21/83, NBC
Lone Ranger, The, 9/15/49–9/12/57, ABC
Loner, The, 9/18/65–4/30/66, CBS

M

Mackenzie's Raiders, 1958–1959, Syndicated
Man Called Shenandoah, A, 9/13/65–9/5/66, ABC
Man from Blackhawk, The, 10/9/59–9/23/60, ABC
Marshal of Gunsight Pass, The, 3/12/50–9/30/50, ABC
Maverick, 9/22/57–7/8/62, ABC
Men from Shiloh, The, 9/9/70–9/8/71, NBC
My Friend Flicka, 2/10/56–5/18/58, CBS

N

Nichols, 9/16/71–8/1/72, NBC
Nine Lives of Elfego Baca, The, (Disney), 1958–1959, ABC
Northwest Passage, 9/14/58–9/8/59

O

Outcasts, The, 9/23/68–9/15/69, ABC
Outlaws, 9/29/60–9/13/62, NBC
Overland Trail, The, 2/7/60–9/11/60, NBC

P

Paradise, 10/27/88–1991, CBS

Q

Quest, The, 9/22/76–12/29/76, NBC

R

Range Rider, The, 1951–1953, Syndicated
Rawhide, 1/9/59–1/4/66, CBS
Rebel, The, 10/4/59–9/12/62, ABC
Restless Gun, 9/23/57–9/14/59, NBC
Rifleman, The, 9/30/58–7/1/63, ABC
Rin-Tin-Tin (see Adventures of)
Riverboat, 9/13/59–1/16/61, NBC
Rough Riders, The, 10/2/58–9/24/59, ABC
Roy Rogers Show, The, 12/30/51–6/23/57, NBC

S

Sergeant Preston of the Yukon, 9/25/55–4/11/64, CBS
Shane, 9/10/66–12/31/66, ABC
Sheriff of Cochise, The, 1956–1957, Syndicated

Shotgun Slade, 1959–1961, Syndicated
Sky King, 9/16/51–10/26/52, NBC
Stagecoach West, 10/4/60–9/26/61, ABC
State Trooper, 1956–1959, Syndicated
Stoney Burke, 10/1/62–9/2/63, ABC
Stories of the Century, 1954–1955, Syndicated
Sugarfoot, 9/17/57–7/3/61, ABC
Swamp Fox, The, 10/23/59–1/15/61, ABC

T

Tales of Texas John Slaughter, 1958–1959, (Disney), ABC
Tales of the Texas Rangers, 9/22/55–5/25/59, CBS
Tales of Wells Fargo, 3/18/57–9/8/62, NBC
Tall Man, The 9/10/60–9/1/62 NBC
Tate, 6/8/60–9/28/60, NBC
Temple Houston, 9/19/63–9/10/64, NBC
Texan, The, 9/29/58–9/12/60, CBS
Tombstone Territory, 10/16/57–10/9/59, ABC
Trackdown, 10/4/57–9/23/59, CBS
26 Men, 1957–1959, Syndicated
Two Faces West, 1960–1961, Syndicated

U

Union Pacific, 1958, Syndicated
U.S. Marshal, 1957–1958, Syndicated

V

Virginian, The, 9/19/62–9/8/71, NBC

W

Wagon Train, 9/18/57–9/1/65, NBC
Wanted Dead or Alive, 9/6/58–3/29/61, CBS
Wells Fargo (see Tales of)
Westerner, The, 9/30/60–12/30/60, NBC
Whiplash, 1961, Syndicated
Whispering Smith, 5/15/61–9/18/61, NBC
Wichita Town, 11/30/59–9/23/60, NBC
Wide Country, 9/20/62–9/12/63, NBC
Wild Bill Hickok (see Adventures of)
Wildside, 3/21/85–4/25/85, (Disney), CBS
Wild, Wild West, The, 9/17/65–9/7/70, CBS
Wrangler, 8/4/60–9/15/60, NBC
Wyatt Earp (see Life and Legend of)

Y

Yancy Derringer, 10/2/58–9/24/59, CBS
Yellow Rose, The, 10/2/83–5/12/84, NBC

Z

Zane Grey Theater, Dick Powell's, 10/5/56–9/20/62, CBS
Zorro, 10/10/57–9/24/59, ABC
Zorro and Son, 4/6/83–6/1/83, CBS

CLUBS AND PUBLICATIONS

The following clubs and publications have requested inclusion in this book.   Some have broad interests in movie and TV cowboy collectibles while others are devoted to specific characters or types of collectibles.   Be sure to include a self-addressed, stamped envelope when writing for additional information.

AMERICAN GAME COLLECTORS ASSN.   Interests include games, puzzles and related playthings.   Publications are *Game Times* and *Game Researchers' Notes*.   Annual fall convention, annual dues $25.   Contact: Secretary, American Game Collectors Assn., 49-H Brooks Ave., Lewiston, ME   04240.

ANTIQUE TOY WORLD.   Monthly publication dedicated to all toys.   Annual subscription $25.   Contact: *Antique Toy World*, PO Box 34509, Chicago, IL   60641.   Phone: (312) 725-0633.

BUFFALO BILL HISTORICAL CENTER.   Located near East Entrance to Yellowstone Park with inclusion of Whitney Gallery of Western Art, Cody Firearms Museum, Plains Indian Museum. Admission $8.00, hours vary. Contact: Public Relations Dept., Box 1000, 720 Sheridan Ave., Cody WY 82414. Phone: (307) 587-4771.

DOUBLE RR-BAR NEWS.   Bimonthly newsletter devoted to Roy Rogers and related memorabilia and collectibles.   Subscriptions $12 for six issues. Contact: Judy or Jim Wilson, J&J Productions, 3438 Scioto Trail, Portsmouth, OH 45662. Phone: (614) 354-2222.

FANDOM DIRECTORY.   Annual reference guide to over 20,000 fans, clubs, publications, conventions, stores, mail-order dealers of movie, TV and related materials. Current edition is 14th year, $18.95 postpaid. Contact: Gary Schlegelmilch, c/o Fandata Publications, 105F Gazebo East Dr., Montgomery, AL 36117. Phone: (205) 279-6665.

FLAKE: THE BREAKFAST NOSTALGIA MAGAZINE.   Published five times a year and featuring cereals, packaging and premiums.   Annual subscription $25 including free 25-word classified ad with subscription.   Contact: *Flake: The Breakfast Nostalgia Magazine*, P.O. Box 481, Cambridge, MA   02140.   Phone: (617) 492-5004.

FRIENDS OF HOPALONG CASSIDY.   Club to perpetuate memory of Hopalong and William Boyd.   Quarterly publication *Hoppy Talk*.   Subscription and annual dues $15.   Annual convention first Saturday in May.   For club information contact: John Spencer, P.O. Box 3674, Frederick, MD   21701.   For subscription contact: Laura Bates, 6310 Friendship Dr., New Concord, OH   43762-9708.   Phone: (614) 826-4850.

HOLLYWOOD STUNTMEN'S HALL OF FAME NEWS.   Illustrated publication about the history of the stunt profession, past and current. Annual subscription $30.00. Associated with Stuntmen's Hall of Fame and Museum, hours Monday-Thursday 10 A.M. to 7 P.M., Saturday-Sunday, noon to 6 P.M. Contact: John Hagner, Founder/Director, P.O. Box 277, Moab UT 84532. Phone: (801) 249-6100.

THE INSIDE COLLECTOR.   Published nine times annually with color photos plus feature articles on popular antiques and collectibles, show and auction reports, calendar of events.   Annual subscription $36.   Contact: *The Inside Collector*, 225 Main St., Suite 300, Northport, NY   11768.   Phone: 1-800-828-1429 (outside New York State) or (516) 261-8337 (within New York State).

NATIONAL BIT, SPUR & SADDLE COLLECTORS ASSN.   Interests include cowboy memorabilia of all types. Quarterly newsletter, calendar of events, roster. Annual dues $20.00, Jan. 1 to Dec. 31. Contact Norma Whitehead, Executive Director, 3604 Galley Rd., Suite 120, Colorado Springs CO 80909. Phone: (719) 591-7136.

NATIONAL COWBOY HALL OF FAME.   Museum of western history, heritage, art and memorabilia representing 17 western states. Located in Oklahoma City, hours Memorial Day through Labor Day 8:30 A.M. to 6 P.M., otherwise September through May 9 A.M. to 5 P.M. Adult admission $6.00, reduced rates for seniors and children. Quarterly publication *Persimmon Hill*, $20.00; annual membership $35.00 includes subscription. Contact: Dana Sullivant, Public Relations Director, NCHF, 1700 Northeast 63rd St., Oklahoma City OK 73111. Phone: (405) 478-2250, Ext. 221.

PAPER COLLECTORS' MARKETPLACE MAGAZINE.   Monthly publication since 1983 for collectors of all types of paper memorabilia.   Annual subscription $17.95.   Contact: *Paper Collectors' Marketplace Magazine*, P.O. Box 128, Scandinavia, WI   54977-0128.   Phone: (715) 467-2379.

SAGEBRUSH JOURNAL.   "The Best Danged Western Newspaper Going!" published bimonthly devoted to "The Real West and The Reel West," B-Westerns, Western collectibles, memorabilia. Annual subscription $15.00 first class mail, $10.00 bulk rate. Associated with Asheville Western Film and Memorabilia Festival held annually the second Thursday through Saturday of November at Ramada Inn West, Asheville, NC, for dealers and public. Contact: Bill Hagen, P.O. Box 6689, Asheville NC 28806. Phone: (704) 253-9808.

TOY SHOP.   Monthly publication on toys and related collectibles.   Annual subscription $23.95.   Contact: Krause Publications, 700 E. State St., Iola, WI   54990.

THE TV COLLECTOR.   Bi-monthly publication for more than 10 years including in-depth articles, interviews, episode guides to past TV series.   Annual subscription $17 (United States), $19 (Canada) includes free ads for subscribers.   Contact: *The TV Collector*, P.O. Box 1088, Easton, MA   02334.   Phone: (508) 238-1179.

WESTERNS & SERIALS.   Club and publication dedicated to B-Westerns and serial chapter play movies of the past.   Quarterly publication of same title.   Annual dues including subscription $16.   Contact: Norman Kietzer, Route 1, Box 103, Vernon Center, MN   56090.   Phone: (507) 540-3677.

THE WRAPPER.   Published eight times annually with ads and articles for non-sport card collectors.   Sample copy $2 plus two stamps.   Annual subscription $21.25.   Contact: *The Wrapper*, 7 Simpson St., Apt. A, Geneva, IL   60134.   Phone: (708) 208-6511.

BIBLIOGRAPHY

Adams, Les, and Rainey, Buck. *Shoot-Em-Ups.* New Rochelle, N.Y.: Arlington House Publishers, 1978.

Barbour, Alan G. *The Thrill of It All.* New York: Collier Books, 1971.

Buxton, Frank, and Owen, Bill. *The Big Broadcast 1920–1950.* New York: Viking Press, 1972.

Dunning, John. *Tune In Yesterday.* Englewood Cliffs, N.J.: Prentice-Hall, Inc., 1976.

Everson, William K. *A Pictorial History of the Western Film.* Secaucus, N.J.: The Citadel Press, 1969.

Fenin, George N., and Everson, William K. *The Western.* New York: Orion Press, 1962.

Halliwell, Leslie. *The Filmgoer's Companion.* 6th ed. New York: Hill and Wang, 1977.

Hake, Theodore L., and Cauler, Robert D. *Six-Gun Heroes.* Des Moines, Iowa: Wallace-Homestead Book Co., 1976.

Hake, Ted. *Hake's Guide To TV Collectibles.* Radnor, Pa.: Wallace-Homestead Book Co., 1990.

Hake, Theodore L. *Hake's Americana & Collectibles Mail and Phone Bid Auction Catalogues.* Nos. 1–124. York, Pa. 1967–1993.

Hardy, Phil. *The Western: The Film Encyclopedia.* New York: William Morrow and Co., 1983.

Heide, Robert, and Gilman, John. *Box-Office Buckaroos.* New York: Abbeville Press, 1982.

Hyams, Jay. *The Life and Times of the Western Movie.* New York: Gallery Books, 1983.

Mathis, Jack. *Valley of the Cliffhangers.* Northbrook, Ill.: Jack Mathis Advertising, 1975.

McNeil, Alex. *Total Television.* New York: Penquin Books, 1984.

Miller, Don. *Hollywood Corral.* New York: Popular Library, 1976.

Miller, Lee O. *The Great Cowboy Stars of Movies & Television.* Westport, Ct.: Arlington House Publishers, 1979.

Parkinson, Michael, and Jeavons, Clyde. *A Pictorial History of Westerns.* New York: Hamlyn Publishing Group Ltd., 1974.

Ragan, David. *Who's Who in Hollywood 1900–1976.* New Rochelle, N.Y.: Arlington House Publishers, 1976.

Rainey, Buck. *The Shoot-Em-Ups Ride Again.* Waynesville, N.C.: The World of Yesterday, 1990.

Summers, Neil. *Official TV Western Book.* 3 vols. Vienna, W. Va.: Old West Shop Publishing, 1987, 1989, 1991.

Weiss, Ken, and Goodgold, Ed. *To Be Continued.* New York: Crown Publishers, 1972.

NAME INDEX

Names of actual persons are listed alphabetically by last name. Names of characters are listed alphabetically by first name. Titles of television shows covered in this book are listed alphabetically in the Table of Contents.

COLLECTIBLES PRICE GUIDES
BY
TED HAKE

The Button Book
(out of print)

Buttons in Sets
with Marshall N. Levin

Collectible Pin-Back Buttons 1896–1986: An Illustrated Price Guide
with Russ King

**The Encyclopedia of Political Buttons 1896–1972; Political Buttons
Book II 1920–1976; Political Buttons Book III 1789–1916**

**The Encyclopedia of Political Buttons: 1991 Revised Prices for
Books I, II, and III**

**Hake's Guide to Advertising Collectibles
100 Years of Advertising From 100 Famous Companies**

**Hake's Guide to Comic Character Collectibles
An Illustrated Price Guide to 100 Years of Comic Strip Characters**

**Hake's Guide to Cowboy Character Collectibles
An Illustrated Price Guide Covering 50 Years of Movie & TV Cowboy Heroes**

**Hake's Guide to Presidential Campaign Collectibles:
An Illustrated Price Guide to Artifacts from 1789–1988**

Hake's Guide to TV Collectibles: An Illustrated Price Guide

Non-Paper Sports Collectibles: An Illustrated Price Guide
with Rogers Steckler

Sixgun Heroes: A Price Guide to Movie Cowboy Collectibles
with Robert Cauler

A Treasury of Advertising Collectibles
(out of print)